# THE HEARTH



## OTHER LATER STUART TAX LISTS AND THE

# ASSOCIATION OATH ROLLS

Compiled by Jeremy Gibson

Federation of Family History Societies

First published 1985 by the

**Federation of Family History Societies,**
c/o The Benson Room, Birmingham and Midland Institute,
Margaret Street, Birmingham B3 3BS, England.

Reprinted with minor amendments and additions, 1986, 1987, 1990.



ISBN 0 907099 34 3

Printed by Parchment (Oxford) Limited

## Acknowledgments

This Guide has been prepared with the approval of the Keeper of Public Records, and I should like to thank him for the facilities with which I was provided and for his permission, and that of the Controller of Her Majesty's Stationery Office, for the use of anything that might be construed as Crown copyright. My thanks go also to the Scottish Record Society and Dr Duncan Adamson for permission to use information on the Scottish Hearth Tax published in S.R.S. vol.9, N.S., 1981; and to Cliff Webb and the Society of Genealogists for permission to use the list of Association Oath Roll class numbers first published in the *Genealogists' Magazine*.

It would have been impossible to contemplate compiling the Guide without Mrs Jane Cox's generous offer of the use of her room at Chancery Lane, where I was able to examine dozens of documents on each of many visits to the Public Record Office. This meant considerable inconvenience to her and various colleagues who had to take turns at invigilation. I am enormously grateful to them all, and to those behind the scenes who had to produce so many records. I hope they will feel the end result has made it worthwhile.

At the Bodleian Library, Colin Harris has constantly sought out obscure publications in response to my telephoned messages (...*Heart Attacks in Hertfordshire*...) and I thank him and his colleagues; it is a privilege and my good fortune to have this wonderful library so accessible and helpful. At the Society of Genealogists, Mr Lawson Edwards has allowed me to borrow the List & Index Society Hearth Tax calendars for months on end, and checked relevant holdings in the library for me, all much appreciated.

Mrs Christine Vialls provided details of her findings on the 'Marriage Tax' in various record offices, and Mr Richard Wall of the Cambridge Group for Population Studies drew my attention to the lists published in *Local Population Studies*, giving me detailed references.

As usual archivists throughout the country have responded to my questionnaires. On this occasion I hope they will be finding useful information on records of their own counties outside their own offices. Others who have helped in various ways include Dr Tom Arkell, Dr D.M. Barratt, Dr J.V. Beckett, Michael Burchall, Janice Capewell, Richard and Celia Cotton, Dr C.M. Fraser, Duncan Harrington, Dr J.D. Marshall, Pat Stevenage, T.L. Stoate and Bill Webster. To all of them I offer my grateful thanks.

**J.S.W.G.**

# Contents

## Introduction

This guide is primarily designed to tell family and local historians of the existence of records of the period 1660-1715, resulting from national legislation, which contain lists of **names**. They are mostly the names of tax-payers (and of those who did not pay the taxes, for various reasons), but the Association Oath Rolls, names of those who swore loyalty to the Crown in 1695, are also included.

It is **not** intended as a definitive guide to the taxation records of the period. Researching family and local history, one seeks the names of individuals. Knowledge of them is usually scanty. Their appearance in some of these lists will add to that knowledge: that they existed at all; that they were alive at that time; that they were living in such a place. Their discovery can lead to other more informative records. But their absence proves little or nothing. It is a lucky dip. With a basic research reason of this nature, there is no need for a prior study of the taxes concerned, on whom they were levied or why. Once names of interest are found, it may well be the researcher will want to find out more about the records in which they appear. On the inside front cover and throughout this Guide there are references to works providing such information, but knowledge of the taxation methods is not a prerequisite of their use.

### The Taxes

The majority of the taxes and their records relate to the reign of Charles II (1660-1685), of which the Hearth Tax generated by far the most (surviving) records, and consequently is the best known and most useful. Others were the 1661 Free and Voluntary Present to the King, Subsidies and Aids, and the Poll Tax. On the accession of William and Mary, the Hearth Tax was repealed (1689), being replaced eventually by the Land Tax and the Window Tax - few records of which survive pre-1715, and these only for the more prosperous - and, for a short time, the 'Marriage Tax', which is of great use and interest to genealogists, but unfortunately only exists for a few places.

Records of the first three are, generally, in the Public Record Office in London (Chancery Lane), and, for the others, as occasional survivals in local record offices. These also sometimes have locally held copies of the Hearth Tax, and of course some have microfilm of nationally held records.

Of the records at the Public Record Office, the Association Oath Rolls are in Class C.213. The tax records are virtually all in Class E.179, Exchequer K.R. Lay Subsidy Rolls, dating from the reign of King John. From 1660 few were either Subsidies or confined to the laiety, but for the purpose of the P.R.O. they are so categorised. The E.179 typescript calendar was published by the List and Index Society, vols. 44 (Beds. - Essex), 54 (Glos. - Lincoln), 63 (London - Somerset), 75 (Staffs. - Yorks.), 87 (Wales, Cinque Ports, Royal Household)(1969-1973), so is available in a few large libraries.

The calendar indicates which tax records include lists of taxpayers ('Names'), and well over a thousand of these documents have been examined and are included in this Guide. Anyone studying E.179 records in any depth should refer to this calendar, as they may well find further references of use to them given there; and there are other Exchequer records relevant to these taxes which I have not attempted to locate or consult.

Against each document in the Public Record Office the reference or call number is shown in **square** brackets. When referring to or ordering up such records, the class number **E.179** (or **C.213** for Oath Rolls) **must** precede this. The figure in **round** brackets refers to the *very* approximate number of persons named. This has been calculated in an attempt to show the extent of any document and thus its likely use to the researcher. It cannot be emphasised too strongly that the figures are based on an extremely cursory examination, especially in the case of the longer records, and may easily be out by many hundreds or even thousands. Anyone requiring such totals must re-examine the documents to reach an accurate figure.

1. *The Free and Voluntary Present to King Charles II.* This was one of the first attempts by Parliament to raise money for the King on his restoration. Although it was voluntary, most of the better-off did subscribe. The money was collected, in the form of promises or cash, generally in towns on market days, in the autumn of 1661, with an occasional 'follow-up' record for slow payers the following year. In some cases occupations are given. Response was variable, often probably depending upon the zeal of the collector. In Surrey just over half of those chargeable in due course under the Hearth Tax subscribed to the 'Present'. In contrast, at Banbury almost as many appear in each: 167 subscribers (ten of whom do not appear in the tax records) to 190 taxpayers. Returns survive for over thirty English and Welsh counties, and this neglected source would repay attention, if only for comparison with the Hearth Tax.

2. *The Hearth Tax.* This was imposed in 1662. Occupiers of houses (rather than owners) were taxed 2s. on each of their hearths, to be collected in two instalments, due at Lady Day (**'L'**)(25th March) and Michaelmas (**'M'**)(29th September). The poor were exempt, but nevertheless were often listed. In later returns (1664-66) they were often shown separately, and in the early 1670s there were special printed forms on which parish officials could list those so exempt.

The first collection was at Michaelmas 1662. That summer parish constables drew up the first lists of householders with the number of hearths each possessed. These paper lists sometimes survive in the E.179 records, and, if sorted and in good repair, are particularly useful. Although the handwriting may be semi-literate at times, the constables had first-hand knowledge of those they were listing, so the names will be at their most accurate. The better-written rolls prepared for the Quarter Sessions, one copy for retention and the other to be forwarded to the Exchequer, are subject to transcription errors and ignorance of the names being copied.

The Hearth Tax continued until 1689, but because of the different authorities responsible at different times, records were returnable to the Exchequer only from Michaelmas 1662 to Lady Day 1666 and again from Michaelmas 1669 to Lady Day 1674. Occasional records outside these dates are found both in the P.R.O. and in local record offices.

In this Guide no discrimination is made between 'assessments' and 'returns'. The assessment was the list drawn up to show what people were expected to pay, the return what they actually did pay - but the assessment was often marked with the payments, thus becoming the return. For the purpose of most users the names and number of hearths are shown in either. For assessments after 1662, and in particular in 1664, the 1662 list was copied for the use of the collectors, and thus a 1664 return will probably list the 1662 householders, annotated to show changes in occupation, increases or decreases of hearths, etc.

The 1662 list is often found to have names of more householders than those of later years, or at least a greater number of hearths assessable. At Banbury there were 190 in comparison with 146 and 138 at the two 1665 returns. However, those of the 1670s may show more, because of greater population, prosperity or efficiency on the behalf of the assessors. Much depends on whether lists of the exempt poor, sometimes as separate exemption certificates, are included.

There are often returns of 'arrears' for 1662-65. These are normally of use only to those studying the tax in depth. Whilst the tax assessments/returns will be in English (possibly with roman numerals for the hearths) and in secretary or other normal contemporary handwriting, these lists of arrears are more formal legal documents, in Latin and in the less familiar court hand. Usually relatively few names are given in any case ('constables' arrears' only list the constables themselves). There are exceptions, when a great number of the poor, who should have been exempt, had in fact been included in the original assessment - such cases will be evident from the figure given for those named.

Single returns for complete counties in England or Wales have now been published for Bedfordshire, Cornwall, Derbyshire, Devon, Dorset, Leicestershire, Norfolk, Oxfordshire, Shropshire, Somerset, Staffordshire, Suffolk, Surrey, Westmorland, Merionethshire and Pembrokeshire. Publication is in progress (with hopes of completion in due course) for Kent, Northumberland and Sussex, and a Nottinghamshire volume is scheduled. Editions comparing all surviving returns have been produced for the Isle of Wight, part of Warwickshire, for the Ealing area of Middlesex and for Banbury in Oxfordshire. The return for Worcester for 1678-80, outside the normal survival period for the tax records, is the most significant of recent volumes for specific places. There are unpublished indexes for Essex, Kesteven in Lincolnshire, Rutland and Warwickshire.

Full bibliographic details of all these are given under the appropriate counties, with comments on their usually excellent and detailed introductions. They will give the interested researcher the information on the tax and its administration which is intentionally omitted here.

3. *Subsidies*. These had been the main means of raising money before the Civil War, and they occur again during the 1660s. Collection was by instalments, so they are difficult to date precisely. Only the wealthier members of the community were affected, gentry, landowners, the more substantial tradesmen. Distinction was made between taxation on goods ('moveables') and land. The amounts paid had become stereotyped and did not relate closely to real wealth, but are still an indication of status. In Banbury forty were assessed compared with four times that number in the Hearth Tax. Surviving records are in the Public Record Office, often in poor repair.

4. *Aids, or Monthly Assessments*. As the counties were responsible for raising fixed quotas, lists of the taxpayers were not forwarded to the Exchequer, and there are rarely any records at the P.R.O. Surviving lists are to be found in city and borough archives, particularly London, Bristol, Shrewsbury, etc.

5. *Poll Tax*. A tax which can list not just the head of the household but also his family and servants. Raised in 1660, 1667, 1678, 1689, 1691, 1694 and 1697. Very rarely survives, mainly in city archives, though the P.R.O. has occasional lists, and, more frequently, lists of defaulters - which, though only relating to very few people, give interesting evidence of mobility.

6. *'Marriage Tax'*, 1695-1706. A tax levied on burials, births and marriages, bachelors over 25 and childless widowers. Effectively can give a census of the whole population, but rarely survives. That for Bristol has been published, and an index to London within the walls. A few others in borough archives, at Leicester, Shrewsbury, Southampton, etc.

7. *Land Tax*. A major tax, instituted about 1692-3 and continuing in some form until the mid 20th century (see *Land Tax Assessments, c.1690-1950*, in this series). Only occasional pre-1715 survivals, in local record offices. Only landowners likely to be listed.

8. *Window Tax*. From 1696. Very few lists, in local record offices, and probably few names in these.

9. *Other Taxes*. Occasional lists for other taxes may have been brought to my attention and so have been included here (i.e., Bedfordshire).

Often it is not clear for what tax the assessment is, so, apart from the Hearth Tax, the categories under which they are shown may be incorrect.

10. *Association Oath Rolls*, 1695. Class C.213 in the Public Record Office. These are described and listed by Cliff Webb in the *Genealogists' Magazine*, vol.21, no.4, December 1983, pp.120-23. This was an oath of loyalty to the Crown to be taken by all office-holders, but open for all to sign if they wished. In some places all males of some age and standing were encouraged to take the Oath and their names enrolled, together with those of defaulters. There are 473 rolls and they have not been individually examined.

Although the Oath was taken in Scotland and probably in Ireland, rolls do not survive at the Public Record Office in Dublin nor at the Scottish Record Office (except for members of Parliament). Locally made lists of signatories in Scotland might be found dispersed among private muniments, court records or burgh records.

The Hearth Tax and Poll Tax in Scotland and the Hearth Tax in Ireland are described under the appropriate sections, pages 58 on.

## The Documents

In the absence of an alternative description, it should be assumed that a document will be a parchment roll, in good repair, and adequately legible - in secretary hand or ordinary later 17th century handwriting. The rolls usually consist of membranes (ms.) around 2-2½ feet in length and 8 inches wide (obviously with many variations). They may hold up to 70-90 entries per column, sometimes more than one column and often written on both sides. They are either stitched just at the head, one on top of another, or head to foot, in one long and often unwieldy roll. Occasionally they have been flattened and then are easier to consult.

Sometimes the collectors were issued with a paper book (particularly the Hearth Tax in 1664) and these, if in good repair, are very much easier to work with.

Comments such as 'VG' relate to the condition and legibility of documents, not to the accuracy or coverage of their content.

The late C.A.F. Meekings, on the staff of the P.R.O., did a great deal of work on the Hearth Tax records, and frequently brief introductions and contents lists by him will be found attached to the documents. These are indicated by the initials 'CAFM'.

*Dating*. Where possible the documents have been given a precise calendar year date, and, with the Hearth Tax, 'L' or 'M' for the Lady Day and Michaelmas collections. These can be confused by returns covering more than one collection, and by bearing dates of the actual time the document and money was sent in, or the assessment was prepared. Sometimes the only date found is a regnal year (fortunately the regnal year for Charles II was from 30th January, so mostly coincides with the calendar year, N.S.), and it is these that are used in the P.R.O.'s list. In these cases the calendar year is shown in brackets.

It is impossible in compiling a Guide of this nature to give much attention to individual documents. Further information from those using them will be very welcome, even if only correction of the number of individuals named or more detail on coverage (and places missing). I will also be very glad to hear of other tax lists for the period, whether in national or local records, and of other transcripts and indexes, published or unpublished. With such a mass of figures and place-names, mistakes are bound to have occurred, and I will most grateful for corrections to references or spellings.

**J.S.W.G.**

## Bedfordshire

Publication

*Hearth Tax* **1671L** [P.R.O. E.179/72/301] (9,500) in Beds. Hist. Record Soc. 16, 1934, as Appx. (pp.65-159) to 'The Rural Population of Bedfordshire 1671-1921', Lydia M. Marshall. Incl. exempt poor and empty houses. Indexed. Accompanying article mainly comparison of C17 and C19 population; no apparent comment on or comparison with other HT records.

Public Record Office [E.179]

***Free and Voluntary Present*, 1661-2**
**County** [243/6](1,250), parchment roll; arrears [243/7](100), paper sheets.

***Hearth Tax*** *(Assessments and returns)*

**1662M. County** [72/297a](5,000). Stodden and Willey hds. missing. Some ms. badly decayed; entries badly faded in parts; modern list of parishes and ms. nos.
**1663L. Westoning** [243/8](1,000). Paper. Constables' returns, those exempt.
**1664M. County** [243/14](5,000). Some decay repaired, variable leg., some fading. Notes against entries relate to 1662M. Modern description and contents list.
**1665L&M. County** [72/298](1,000). Variations. Valuable notes on reasons for not paying, i.e. in prison, no distress to be taken. Dated 12 Apr 1666.
**(1666). Stodden, Clifton, Barford, Wixhamtree hds.** [243/9](5,000). Paper, repaired, bound. Annotated.
**Flitton, Manshead, Biggleswade, Redbornstoke hds.** [243/10](2,500). Paper book, repaired, annotated. VG.
**1671L. County** [72/301](9,500). Published.
**1671(L?). County** [72/302](9,500). Badly decayed; otherwise legibility adequate.
*(Arrears)*
**1664L. County** [370/1](30). Latin.
**1663-4.** [358]. Miscellaneous.

***Subsidies***
**(1660). Wixhamtree, Clifton, Biggleswade hds.** [72/296](400).
**1661. Manshead hd.** [72/297](900). Parts badly faded, variable legibility.
**(1673). Barford, Stodden, Willey hds.** [72/306](500). Poor legibility.

***Association Oath Rolls*, 1695** [C.213]
[2] **County**; [3] **Bedford.**

Bedfordshire Record Office,
County Hall, Bedford MK42 9AP.

***Hearth Tax***
**1665.** Part of **Manshead hd.**: Billington, Houghton Regis, Toddington, Tilsworth, Harlington, Totternhoe, Milton Bryan, Woburn [AD 3350 pp.15-18].
**c.1683.** Northill, incl. the hamlets of Ickwell, Over or Upper Caldecote, Nether or Lower Caldecote, Thorncote, Hatch, Brook End, Beeston [HY 823].

***Poll Tax***
**1689-90.** Renhold [PO 14 p.19-20].
**1694.** Aspley Guise [HW 41].

***Aids***
**1693.** Cranfield [LL 7/3]; Maulden [LL 7/4].

***Ship Money***
**1677.** Renhold [PO 14 p.8]; Cople [ABP/W 1684/20].

***Weekes' Tax***
**1707, 1715.** Renhold [PO 14 p.40].

***Certainty Money***
**1712.** Houghton Conquest [R4/324].

***Land Tax***
**1697, 1706.** Renhold [PO 14 p.39].

## Berkshire

Publications

*Hearth Tax*, for **Reading St Mary** and **St Giles, 1664M** [P.R.O. E.179/76/460, formerly 76/458], **St Laurence and Whitley 1663M** [243/25], **Caversham** (formerly Oxon.) **1662M** [255/4 (Oxon)](total 510 names), in *The Hearth Tax for Reading and Caversham 1662-3*, transcribed and edited by Edgar Powell, 1913.

*Hearth Tax*, **Uffington, Baulking, Woolstone, Kingston Lisle, Fawler, 1663M** [P.R.O. E.179/243/25] in *Berkshire Tracts 1*, transcribed by J.E. Little.

*Hearth Tax*, **Wantage 1663M** [P.R.O. E.179/243/25](144) in *Berkshire FHS Jnl.* **7**, 4 (Summer 1982).

Public Record Office [E.179]

***Free and Voluntary Present*, 1661-2**
**County** [243/21](2,500-3,000). Varying size rolls.

***Hearth Tax*** *(Assessments and returns)*

**1662M. County** [243/24](9,000). Constables' returns, paper, bound, VG.
**Morton hd.** (N and S divs.) and **Newbury** (town)[243/27](2,000-3,000). Constables' assessments. Paper.
**Ganfield hd.** [367/1](25). Shillingford only.
**1663M. County** [243/25](9,000). Constables' returns, paper, loose.
**Ock hd.** [75/381](365). Constables' returns, paper. Including exempt poor. Kilns listed for Sutton Courtenay. Dated 6 June 1664.
**Kintbury Eagle hd.** [75/400](250). Constables' returns, paper. Include exempt poor for Kintbury, Almsbury(?). Dated 5 March 1663 and 1 Nov 1664.
**1664L. County** [243/26](5,000). Constables' returns, paper, bound in 3 books. VG.
**1664M. County** [76/460](6,500). Patchy. Parts adequately legible, part badly faded or decayed; partially repaired. Modern contents list of hundreds.
**1663-64. County** [358]. Very many loose paper returns by constables, unsorted.

***Subsidies***
**No date. Beynhurst hd.** [75/379](150). Poor condition and legibility, faded in parts.
**Faircross hd.** [76/459](500). Badly faded in part.
**? hd.** [243/28](120). Incl. Shefford, Chaddleworth cum Woolley, North and South Fawley cum Whatcombe, Budcombe Basset. Bad condition, poor legibility. Possibly Poll Tax, not Subsidy.

***Poll Tax***
**(1661). Cookham hd.** [243/22](100).
**(1667).** Newbury, Bagnor, Welford, Speenhamland. Certificates of defaulters [76/449b](19).
**1678 May.** Aldermaston [76/454](130). Bad handwriting.
**June.** Faringdon, Shrivenham, Ganfield, Wantage, Lamborne [76/456](106). Collectors' names only.
**June.** Kintbury Eagle and Compton [76/455](104). Collectors' names only.
**July.** Reading and Theale hds. [76/457] (57). Collectors' names only.



***Association Oath Rolls*, 1695** [C.213]

[4] **County**; [5] **Vale of Berkshire**;
[6] **Wantage**; [7] **New Windsor**;
[8] **Reading**; [9] **Wallingford**;
[10] **Abingdon**; [11] **Newbury**;
[12] **Maidenhead**; [13] **Wokingham**;
[14] **Easthampstead.**

Berkshire Record Office, Shire Hall, Shinfield Park, Reading RG2 9XD.

***Hearth Tax***

**1663M.** Photocopies of P.R.O. E.179/243/25 [T/A 17/] for:
1 Newbury; 2 Abingdon; 3 Maidenhead; 4 Clewer; 5 New Windsor; 6 Whistley-in-Hurst; 7 Compton, East and West; 8 East Ilsley; 9 Yattendon; 10 Speenhamland; 11 Brightwalton; 12 Hinton Waldrist; 13 Cumnor, Wootton, Witham, North and South Hinksey (incl. Botley); 14 **Hd of Hormer**: Abingdon (Sandford, Northcourt, Shippon), Sunningwell, Kennington, Radley (incl. Thrupp), Besselsleigh, Grandpont; 15 **Hd of Kintbury Eagle** (north side) incl. Letcombe Regis and Bassett; 16 Sonning town; 17 Wallingford; 18 Winterbourne and Chieveley; 19 Maidenhead; 20 Wantage, Grove, Charlton; 21 Frilford, Lyford, East Hanney, Draycott Moor, Goosey, Fyfield, Garford, Appleton (incl. Eaton), Marcham, Kingston Bagpuize, Tubney; 22 Wokingham; 23 Hungerford; 24 Sandford-in-the-Vale.
**Goosey.** Photocopies of **1662M**, P.R.O. E.179/243/24 [T/A 35.3] and **1664M** E.179/76/460 [T/A 35.4].

***Land Tax**, etc.*
**1679- .** Brightwalton.
**1704.** Watchford, Woolhampton.

Society of Genealogists, 14 Charterhouse Buildings, Goswell Rd, London EC1M 7BA.

Snell Collection, vol.17 (MS) has indexed transcripts of *Hearth Tax* **1663-4** [P.R.O. E.179/243/25] for about 90 parishes.

## Buckinghamshire

Publications

**Langley Marish** *Hearth Tax* **1663M** (135), *Heritage* (Windsor/Slough FHS) **4**,3 (1981).

**Great Hampden**, *Poll Tax* **1660**, *Subsidy/Aid*, **1668, 1673** [Bucks R.O. D/LE/17], *Origins* (Bucks FHS) **9**, 2 & 3 (1985).

**Buckinghamshire**, continued

Public Record Office [E.179]

***Free and Voluntary Present*, 1661-2**

**County** [80/333](3,000). Paper book.

***Hearth Tax*** *(Assessments and returns)*

**1662M. Ashendon hd.** [80/354](900). Much decayed at foot and consequently patchy legibility.

**Aylesbury** (3 hds.)[80/348](500). Many entries lost from decay, poor legibility, bad condition but repaired.

**Buckingham** (3 hds.)[244/16](1,000). Decayed but repaired. Part badly faded or decayed, part fair leg.

**Burnham hd.** [80/350](1,000). Repaired after bad decay. Hearths mainly lost; some names legible.

**Cottesloe hd.** [80/352](1,000). Repaired but mostly illegible.

**Desborough hd.**[80/345](70). Bad condition and legibility, unfit for production.

**Newport** (3 hds.)[80/349](3,000). Decayed but repaired. Part good legibility, part faded or lost.

**Stoke hd.** [80/347](900). Decayed but repaired. Some bad fading. Modern list of contents.

**1662M-1664L. County** [244/11](375). Constables' returns, paper.

**County** [80/351]. Variations schedule. Repaired but very poor and illegible.

**1663-4.** [358]. Stray constables' paper returns: (north) Edgcott, Twyford (2), Shalstone, Water Stratford, Tingewick, Preston Cowley, Thorndon, Turweston, Barton Hartshorn, Steeple Claydon, Hillesden, Westbury, Marsh Gibbon; (south) Aston Clinton, Buckland, Borton cum Broughton, Farnham Royal (2), Waterside in Chesham, Chalfont St Peter, Taplow, Dorney, Bouny/Boueney, Burnham.

**1672. Aylesbury hd.**, Haddenham, Little Kimble [244/12](320). Constables' return, paper book.

**?1672. Aylesbury hd.** [244/15](600). Paper book, similar to 244/12.

**No date. Buckingham hd.**(part) [367/1] (?100). Fragment. Bad condition.

*(Arrears)*

**1674L. County** [244/13](300). Latin.

***Subsidies***

**1663 Sep. Burnham hd.**[80/335](200). Repaired but most names partially lost through decay.

**Nov. Desborough hd.** [244/10](65). Certificates of residence.

**Buckinghamshire**: P.R.O., *Subsidies*, ctd.

**(1664). Aylesbury** (3 hds.)[80/336](500). Repaired. Some entries lost from decay; faded in parts poor legibility.

**Chiltern** (3 hds.)[80/338](1,000). 1 ms. badly faded (Durney and Burnham), but otherwise good legibility and condn.

**Cottesloe** (3 hds.)[80/337](200). Faded and decayed, repaired. Some parts leg.

**Newport** (3 hds.)[80/334](1,500). Faded in parts, poor legibility.

***Association Oath Rolls*, 1695** [C.213]

[15-16] **County**; [17] Deputy Lieutenants and Militia Officers;

[18] **Buckingham**; [19] **Chipping** (High) **Wycombe**; [20] **Aylesbury**;

[21] **Amersham**; [22] **Great Marlow**;

[23] **Wendover**.

Buckinghamshire Record Office,
County Hall, Aylesbury HP20 1UA

***Subsidies or Aids***

**Aylesbury hds.**, 1665 [D138/22/3]; 1668 [D/LE/17/8]; 1673 [D/LE/17/9] (Gt Hampden 1668 and 1673 published).

***Poll Tax***

**Aylesbury hds.**, 1660 [D/LE/17/3] (Great Hampden published).

**Stoke hds.**, 1694, 1698-9 [D/W/89-90].

**Cheddington**, 1694 [D12/78].

***Land Tax***, *etc.*

**West Wycombe**: 1689,1700,1703,1705,1707, 1709,1712 [PR 227/28/1].

***Marriage Tax***

Liberty of **Shipton Lee** in Quainton, 1696 [PR.169/28/6].

**Quainton**, 1702 [PR.169/28/6].

**Great Brickhill**, various [PR.25/1/2].

## Cambridgeshire and Isle of Ely

Publications

Descriptive articles on the *Hearth Tax*, in the relevant volumes of the *V.C.H.*, by CAFM, with details of P.R.O. documents in vol.4, p.272. Analyses of totals but no names.

'Family History from Records of Property: *Hearth Tax*'. Janet Hurst, *Jnl. Cambo FHS*, **2**, 5 (Feb 1980).

*Cambridgeshire Subsidy Rolls, 1250-1695* by W.M. Palmer (Norwich, 1912, reprinted from *The East Anglian*, 1898-1909), incl. lists for **Shingay-cum-Wendy**, 1660, 1661, pp.28-9, and for **Melbourn**, 1672, p.31.

**Cambridgeshire**: Publications, continued

*Hearth Tax*, **1674, Melbourn** and **Meldreth**, [presumably P.R.O. E.179/326/10](216), in 'Some C17 Inhabitants of South-West Cambs.', Janet Hurst, *Jnl. Cambs FHS*, **3**, 2 (May 81), reprinted from articles in the *Congregational Magazine*, Jan 1895, reprinted in *A Nonconformist Bicentenary Memorial* (Cambridge Central Library).

Public Record Office [E.179]
(asterisked items are also on microfilm at the Cambridgeshire C.R.O., Cambridge)

***Free and Voluntary Present*, 1661-2**
**County** [84/433]*(3,000). In 13 separate rolls (each separate ms. inside), by hundreds, etc.

***Hearth Tax*** *(Assessments and returns)*

**1662M. County** [84/436]*(9,000). Enrolled assessment listing all bound to pay (some subsequently exempt). Fewer names than later rolls.
**Whittlesey** [244/24](400). Paper book, repaired.
**1664M/1665. County** [84/437]*(17,000). Enrolled, thorough revision of 1662M. Almost as comprehensive as 1674L. Numerous comments, removals, new entries, those exempt. VG, but imperfect.
**1666L. County** [244/22]*(17,200). Returns, paper books made after tax had been collected. Headings of 'Paid' and 'Unpaid'.
**1670M. County** [375/27, formerly 244/25] (5,000). Introduction by CAFM. Incl. Cambridge town, Ely, Wichford, Wisbech, Armingford, Chesterton hds. Much decay, repaired, and fading, but legible and good in parts. Cambridge mainly illeg. Ely much decayed. Other hds. variable.
**1671M-1673L. County** [244/26](300). Fragment of roll, bad condition and leg.
**1674L. County** [244/23]*(13,500). Lists made by sub-collectors. Divided into taxpayers and those exempt by certificate. Fair copy; ms. all bound at top, easy to use. Transcript at SofG.
*(Exemption certificates)*
**1671M. Armingford hd.** [326/2](740). Printed certificates, repaired and bound. Modern contents list.
**1672/1673L. Chesterton, Northstow, Papworth hds.** [84/440]*(3,500). Repaired and bound, modern contents list.
**1674L. County** [326/10](200). Printed certificates, much decayed but repaired, bound. Modern contents list.

**Cambridgeshire**: P.R.O., continued

***Subsidies***
**(1663). County** [244/21](500). Fragment, bad condn., parts leg. but most illeg.
**(1664). Chesterton, Northstow, Papworth hds.** [84/435](300).

***Poll Tax***
**(1660). Armingford, Longstowe, Thriplow, Wetherley hds.** [83/429](500). Poor condition and legibility.
**Flendish, Staine, Staploe, Thriplow, Wetherley hds.** [83/430](70). Names of constables only.
**Flendish hd.** [83/431](100).
**Isle of Ely** [83/432](100). Names of collectors and constables only.
**Staine, Whittlesford hds.** [244/20](250). One membrane damaged by damp.
**1678. Chilford hd.** [84/444,446]*(85). Part faded; incomplete.
**Longstowe hd.** [84/445]*(250). Decayed and faded, poor condition and leg.

***Association Oath Rolls*** [C.213]
[24] **Cambridgeshire**; [25] **Cambridge**; [26] **Isle of Ely**.

Cambridgeshire Record Office, Cambridge.

Microfilm of asterisked P.R.O. holdings.

***Hearth Tax***
Original: **1662M. Guilden Morden.**
Transcript: **Cambridge** borough, **1664, 1674.**
***Subsidies***
Littleport, 1662-3(4), 1663(2), 1671.
***Poll Tax***
Comberton, 1692.
***Assessments for Aids and Taxes***
Bassingbourn, 1692, 1698, 1711, 1712.
***Trophy Tax for the drums and colours***
Bassingbourn, 1690, 1694, 1706, 1715.
***Land Tax***
Bassingbourn, 1715; Comberton, 1707; Linton, 1694; Meldreth, 1699-1720.

Society of Genealogists

***Hearth Tax*: 1662M.** Whittlesey.
**1674L. County**. Indexed transcript.

## Cheshire

Publications

*Northwich Hundred. Poll Tax* ***1660*** *and Hearth Tax* ***1664***, Lancs. & Ches. R.S., 119 (1979), ed. G.O. Lawton. Indexed. *Poll Tax* [P.R.O. E.179/244/30](5,756); *Hearth Tax* [E.179/86/145](2,585), separated into chargeable and exempt.

**Cheshire**: Publications, continued

*Hearth Tax*, **Chester, 1665M** [P.R.O. E.179/86/146](1,500), in 'Hearth Tax Returns for the City of Chester, 1664-5', ed. F.C. Beazley, Lancs. & Ches. R.S., **52** (*Miscellanies*, vol.5), 1906. Indexed. Arranged by ward. Includes changes and additions since 1662, also exempt poor. Short introduction.

*Hearth Tax* returns for **Eddisbury** and **Wirral hds.** are in volumes of *Cheshire Sheaf*, series 3. This was a monthly, bound and indexed in annual volumes. The indexes include names in the HT (take care not to consult the adjacent but separate indexes to apprenticeship indentures). HT lists are scattered through the issues, in numbered sections, also listed in annual contents lists.
**Wirral hd., 1663L** [P.R.O. E.179/244/35 (compared against E.179/86/145)] in vols. 8 (1910) and 9 (1912), secs. 1535-2097.
**Eddisbury hd., Western div., 1663L** [E.179/244/34] in vol.7 (1909), 1222-1347.
**Eddisbury hd., Eastern and Western divs., 1664L** [E.179/86/145], in vols.11-13 (1914-16), secs. 2452-2650, 2806-3243.
Part of **Broxton hd., 1663L** [E.179/244/34] is in vol.14 (1917), not apparently completed, and **note** that this transcript excludes single hearth households.

**Lymm, High Legh, Thelwall, 1673L&M, 1674L** (230), in '*Hearth Tax* Assessments of Lymm', M.N. Jackson, *North Cheshire FH*, **5**, 2 (May 1978), pp.46-49.

Public Record Office [E.179]

***Free and Voluntary Present*, 1661-2**
**Broxton hd.** [244/32a](1,250).
**Bucklow hd.** [86/159](1,000).
**Eddisbury hd.** [244/32](1,500).
**Nantwich hd.** [244/31](1,200). Decayed and faded in parts.

***Hearth Tax*** *(Assessments and returns)*
(* = microfilm at Cheshire R.O.)

**1662M. County** [86/141](?5,000). Bad condition and legibility.
**1663L.** High constables' books, paper, for **Broxton** (1,750), **Eddisbury** (1,250), **Macclesfield** (3,000) **hds** [244/34]*; **Wirral hd.** (1,150)[244/35]*. Part pubd.
**1663L-1664L. Chester** [86/143]*(1,250). By ward. Incl. decreases and exempt.
**1664L. County** [86/145]*(24,000). VG, fair copy parchment book in sections. Chargeable and exempt separated. Eddisbury, Northwich hds. published.
**Chester** [86/142]*(1,250). By ward, exempt listed.

**Cheshire**: P.R.O., *Hearth Tax*, continued

**1665M Broxton** [86/149]*(2,250), **Nantwich** [86/148]*(2,400), **Northwich** [86/150]*(3,000), **Eddisbury and Wirral hds.** [244/37]*(5,000). Fair copy parchment books. Incl. changes in occupation, those exempt.
**Chester** [86/146]. Published, see left.
**County** [358](1,200). Paper. Defaulters, tabulated to show reasons. VG.
**1671M. County** [16/153](1,250). Parchment book, annotated. Good.
**1674L. County** [86/155]*(10,000). VG. Parchment books.
*(Exemption certificates)*
**1670, 1672. County** [86/152](4,000 for each year). VG, repaired and bound, mainly printed forms, in two books.
**1674. County** [326/5](3,000). Printed paper forms, bound.
**Chester** [326/4](371). Printed paper forms, bound.
*(Arrears)*
**1663M. County** [370/8](100). Latin.
**1663. Chester** [370/9,10](50 & 50). Latin.
**1664L. County** [86/144]*(75). Latin.

***Subsidies*** (* = m'film at Cheshire R.O.)
**1663. Wirral hd.** [244/33]*(200). Parchment sheets, bad condn. and legibility.
**1660-69. Broxton hd.** [86/151](1,000). Fragments, some very bad, some legible.

***Poll Tax***
**1660. Bucklow hd.** [272/40](400). Very bad condn., unfit for production.
**Chester** [244/29](2,400). Paper book.
**Northwich** [244/30](5,756). Published.

***Association Oath Rolls*, 1695** [C.213] [27-28] **County**; [29-31] **Chester** city; [32] **Congleton.**

Cheshire Record Office, Duke Street, Chester CH1 1RL.

Microfilm of P.R.O. *Hearth Tax* holdings as asterisked, 1663-5, 1673-4.

Chester City Record Office, Town Hall, Chester CH1 2HJ.

***Hearth Tax*** [CAS]
**1672. Chester** (whole city).

***Subsidies/Aids*** [CAS]
**1662.** Some wards.
**1664-5, 1666. Chester** city.
**1673, 1677, 1679, 1685, 1692, 1699,** ?whole city, or at least some wards.

***Poll Tax*** [CAS]
**1662-3.** St Giles' ward; St John's parish.
**1692, 1694, 1698.** City (incomplete).

## Cornwall

Publications

*Cornwall Hearth and Poll Taxes, 1660-1664: Direct Taxation in Cornwall in the Reign of Charles II*, ed. and pub. by T.L. Stoate, 1981. Full transcripts of *Hearth Tax* **1664M** [P.R.O. E.179/244/44], *Free and Voluntary Present 1661* [E.179/244/41], and *Poll Tax* **1660, Kerrier hd., East hd.** (northern div.) [E.179/244/39], **Powder hd.** (eastern div.) [E.179/244/40]. All indexed. Detailed introduction and description of all P.R.O. E.179 records.

**St Constantine** parish *Poll* and *Hearth Taxes* [as above] and undated *Hearth Tax* returns [P.R.O. E.179/244/45](74) are published in Devon and Cornwall Record Society, No.9, 1910. Indexed.

Public Record Office [E.179]

***Free and Voluntary Present*, 1661-2**
**County** [244/41](1,000). Published.

***Hearth Tax*** *(Assessments and returns)*

**1662M. County** [89/356](9,000). Decayed and repaired, ms. stitched at top. Bad condn. and leg. Intro. and contents list. Trigg and Penwith hds. missing. Virtually duplicated in 244/44, 1664M.
**1664M. County** [244/44]. Published.
**1666L. Truro, St Just, Creed** [244/46] (200). Paper, repaired and bound.
**1666M. Pyder hd.** [244/42](400). Paper, constables' returns, bound.
*(Arrears)*
**1662M** [370/12,13](80 and 50). Latin, mainly names of constables.
**1664-66** (for 1662M)[370/14](150). Latin. (for 1664L)[370/15](160). Latin.

***Subsidies***
**1663. Penwith hd.** [89/348](350).
**Pyder hd.** [89/346 and 244/43](350).
**West hd.** [89/347](750).

***Poll Tax***
**1660. Kerrier** and **East** (northern divn.) **hds.** [244/39](8,000). Published. Paper, bound, complete.
**Powder hd.** (eastern divn.)[244/40] (5,500). Published. Paper, bound.
**Pyder hd.** [89/345](1,000). Bad leg.
**(?1692).** St Agnes, part of St Breock in Pyder [276/73a](150). Variable.

***Assessment or General Aid***
**1689. Pyder hd.** [244/47](1,000). Paper. Incl. Columb Major, Padstow, Newlyn, St Agnes, St Ervan, St Breock, St Enoder.
**Pyder hd.** [369/23](110). Paper, repaired. Perranzabuloe, Little Colan.

**Cornwall**: P.R.O., continued

***Association Oath Rolls*, 1695** [C.213]
[33-35] **County**, Grand Jury, tinners; [36-37] **Launceston**; [38] **Liskeard**; [39] **Lostwithiel**; [40] **Truro**; [41] **Bodmin**; [42] **Helston**; [43] **Saltash**; [44] **Camelford**; [45] **West Looe**; [46] **Grampound**; [47] **East Looe**; [48] **Penryn**; [49] **Tregony**; [50] **Bossiney**; [51] **St Ives**; [52] **Fowey**; [53] **St German**; [54] **St Michael**; [55] **St Mawes**; [56] **Callington**; [57] **Falmouth**; [58] **Penzance**; [59] **Marazion**; [464] **Scilly Isles**.

## Cumberland

Public Record Office [E.179]

***Free and Voluntary Present*, 1661-2**
**County** [90/73](1,000).

***Hearth Tax*** *(Assessments and returns)*

**1662L. County** [90/77](7,500). Some ms. torn and Carlisle at end, several ms. wanting. See also 245/3.
**1662. County** [245/3](5,000). Small parchment ms., half badly decayed.
**(1673). County** [90/74](10,000). Much decayed, but repaired and flattened. Parts easily legible, other parts faded and/or decayed.
**1673M/1674L. County** [90/76](12,500). Legibility generally good, but some poor. Includes exempt poor.
**(?year).** [90/78](350). Fragments, incl. Braithwaite, Eskdale, Wastdale, Harrington, Briashat, Workington, Stainbarne. Varying condn. and legibility.
*(Exemption certificates)*
**1673. County** [326/6](3,000). Printed paper forms, bound.

***Subsidies***
**(1663). County** [245/1](210). Poor condn.
**1663** Feb. **Carlisle** [245/2](16). Paper.
**1664** Apr. **Allerdale ward** [90/75](33).

***Association Oath Rolls*, 1695** [C.213]
[60-61] **County**, nonconformist ministers; [62] **County**, Lord Lieutenant, etc.; [63] **Carlisle**; [64] **Cockermouth**; [65] **Whitehaven**.

Cumbria Record Office,
The Castle, Calisle CA3 8UR.

***Hearth Tax***
**c.1664. County** (photostat copy).
**1673. Carlisle** (modern transcript).

## Derbyshire

Publications

*Hearth Tax*, **County, 1662-70** [exact coverage and original records shown below], in *Derbyshire Hearth Tax Assessments, 1662-70*, ed. David G. Edwards with an introduction incorporating material by the late C.A.F. Meekings, Derbyshire Record Society, vol.7, 1982.
**Appletree hd.** (Spondon and Borrowash only), **1662M** [P.R.O. E.179/93/378];
**Appletree hd.** (remainder of hd.), **1664L** [P.R.O. E.179/94/405]. Incl. exempt poor.
**Repton and Gresley hd., 1662M** (most of hd.)[P.R.O. E.179/245/7]; (Winshill, Repton, Rosliston, Coton only)[P.R.O. E.179/94/378].
**Repton and Gresley hd., 1664L** (Walton upon Trent only)[P.R.O. E.179/245/10]. Incl. exempt poor.
**High Peak, Morleston and Litchurch, Scarsdale,** and **Wirksworth hds., 1670** [Derby Central Library, Derbyshire Collection, DC 9953-56].
Fully indexed.
The admirable introduction gives a very readable explanation of the mechanics of the collection of the tax, and the complexities of dating the returns. Table 1 shows the principal surviving Hearth Tax records for the county, in the P.R.O. and in Derby Central Library, with an indication of completeness and/or legibility, date and hundred. Pp.xviii-xxxv describe these in detail, document by document, and forms the basis for the brief notes below.

*Marriage Tax*, **Melbourne, 1695** (660), *Jnl. Derbys. Arch. and Nat. Hist. Soc.*, **7** (1885), pp.1-30, with an introduction by R.E. Chester Waters. Indexed.

Public Record Office [E.179]

***Free and Voluntary Present*, 1661-2 County** [245/6](4,000).

***Hearth Tax*** *(Assessments and returns)*

**1662M. County** [94/378](10,000). Exchequer duplicate. Appletree, Scarsdale hds. defective; Derby largely missing. Decayed, repaired, condition and legibility generally poor. Spondon and Borrowash; Winshill, Repton, Rosliston and Coton published, see above.
**Appletree hd.** [245/8](2,000). Exchequer duplicate, paper book, copy of 94/378 (only hd. surviving), but made for 1664M.



**1662M/1664L. County** [245/7](10,000). Constables' paper returns, as 1662M, but made or confirmed in Oct 1664. Includes three arrears schedules. Bound as book. Introduction by CAFM. Easy to use (lengthy description in D.R.S.7, pp.xix-xxiii). Repton and Gresley hd. publ. M'film in Derby Lib.
**1664L. County.** Exchequer duplicate. Exempt poor shown. Split into hds. with separate references:
**Derby, Morleston and Litchurch hd.** [94/401](2,000). Outer ms. faded, otherwise perfect. Markeaton missing.
**Appletree hd.** [94/405](1,800). Dorse of m.11 and tails of mm.3 and 4 rubbed, otherwise perfect. Borrowash and Spondon missing, Shottle and Postern illegible. Published, see left. Microfilm at Derby Central Library.
**Scarsdale hd.** [94/400](3,600). Mostly perfect. Possibly 1m. missing.
**Wirksworth hd.** [94/402](2,610). Perfect. Bonsall and Newton Grange missing.
**High Peak hd.** [94/403](3,500). Some 80 entries illegible (mm.13,14,16,17), otherwise perfect.
**Repton and Gresley hd** [245/10](1,200). Decay, repaired, four ms. illegible in parts. Some ms. lost. Defective. Walton on Trent published, see left.
For **1670**, see Derbyshire Central Library, page 16.
**1672. Scarsdale hd.** [94/394](3,500). Exchequer duplicate. Places arranged alphabetically, preceded by Chesterfield; missing: Barlow, Beauchief, Calow, Tibshelf and Oxcroft, Walton, Wingerworth.
**Appletree hd.** [245/9/1](1,800). Places arranged alphabetically. 2ms. missing, others partly illegible.
**High Peak hd.** [245/9/2](2,650). Constablewicks in alphabetical order, but places within them in no particular order. 3ms. missing, others partly illegible.
**Wirksworth hd.** [245/9/3](1,600). Places arranged in alphabetical order, Ashbourne to Wensley and Snitterton. Final m. missing.
*(Exemption certificates)* **(County)**
**1670-1** [326/7](2,500); **1672** [326/12] (250)(not mentioned in D.R.S. 7); **1673-4** [326/8](500). Paper, some on printed forms, 84 in 326/7, allocated to hds. in D.R.S. **7**, 46 in 326/8. Each lot bound together. Do not add any names to 1670 return [DC 9953-6].

**Derbyshire**: P.R.O., continued

***Subsidy***

**1664/5. Repton and Gresley hd.** [94/377] (130). Also 12 certs. of residence.

***Association Oath Rolls*, 1695** [C.213] [66] **County**; [67] **Derby** town.

Derby Central Library, Derbyshire Collection, The Wardwick, Derby DE1 1HS.

***Hearth Tax*** *(originals)*

**1670. County** (Appletree, Repton & Gresley hds. missing). Paper books, originally the collectors' records. Complete and in good condition. Published, D.R.S.**7**.

**Wirksworth hd.** [DC 9953].

**Scarsdale hd.** [DC 9954].

**High Peak hd.** [DC 9955].

**Morleston and Litchurch hd.** [DC 9956].

*(microfilms)*

**1662M. Repton and Gresley hd.** [P.R.O. E.179/245/7]. Published, see page 15.

**1664L. Appletree hd.** [P.R.O. E.179/94/405] Published, see page 15.

Derbyshire Record Office, County Offices, Matlock, Derbys. DE4 3AG.

***Various Tax Papers** for **wapentake of Wirksworth** and parishes (including Ashbourne) within the hundred* [Chandos-Pole-Gell papers, D258]

**1679, 1680**: assessments for disbanding the army [6/12, S/6].

**1677–78**: parish assessments for money to build 30 war ships [28/6, 33; 29/13; 56/40].

**1673–74**: assessments for his majesty's extraordinary occasions [24/11; 58/29; S/5].

**1678, 1689**: *Poll Tax*, Wirksworth wapentake [56/41; 48/10].

**1705–1719**: occasional *Land Tax* assessments for parishes within wapentake.

**17th century** (unspecified): other assessments, not been possible to tie to individual taxes.

Nottinghamshire Record Office, County House, High Pavement, Nottingham NG1 1HR.

***Free and Voluntary Present*, 1661–2**

**Scarsdale hd.** [DD.3P 2/1]. List of subscribers taken at Alfreton, Bolsover, Dronfield and Chesterfield. 8ms.

**High Peak hd.** [DD.3P 2/2]. List of subscribers taken at Bakewell, Tideswell and Chapel en le Frith. 4ms.

Sheffield Central Library, Archives Department, Surrey St, Sheffield S1 1XZ.

*Marriage Tax*, **1695, Darley** [Bar D.728].

## Devon

Publications

*Devon Hearth Tax Return: Lady Day 1674*, ed. and pub. T.L. Stoate, 1982. Full transcript of **1674L** [P.R.O. E.179/245/17](22,919). Also includes an index to places in the 1664L return [E.179/102/530], and an introduction discussing and analysing the records of the Hearth Tax surviving for the county. Indexed.

*Exeter in the Seventeenth Century: Tax and Rate Assessments, 1602–1699*, ed. W.G. Hoskins, Devon and Cornwall Record Society, N.S., vol.2, 1957, includes *Poll Tax*, **1660** [Exeter City Archives, Box 4; P.R.O. duplicate, E.179/102/482] (6,845); *Hearth Tax*, **1671M** [Exeter City Archives Misc. Rolls No.74; P.R.O. duplicate E.179/102/534](2,400). Indexed.

Public Record Office [E.179]

***Free and Voluntary Present*, 1661–2**

**North Tawton hd.** [102/519](159). Flat. Fading in parts.

***Hearth Tax*** *(Assessments and returns)* (microfilm copies are in the West Country Studies Library, Exeter Central Library)

**1662M. Exeter** city [102/520](800). Poor condition and legibility.

**Coleridge hd.** (part of Charleton Slapton, fragment of Chivelstone), **Roborough hd.** (part of Vaulterhome tithing, part of Weston Peverel), **Cliston hd.** (part of ?Broad Clyst, Butterleigh, part of Whimple)[375/13] (140). Fragmentary remains of County assessment.

**1664L. County** [102/530](?4,000). TS intro. and contents. 37 out of 150 ms. remaining. Much decayed, repaired, much illegible, but parts OK. Key to parishes in *Devon Hearth Tax 1674*.

**1671M. Exeter** city [102/534]. Duplicate at Devon R.O., published in *Exeter in the Seventeenth Century*.

**1672M–1673L. Tiverton** town and parish [245/19](320).

**1674L. County** [245/17]. Published, see above.

*(Arrears)*

**1662M.** Rackenford, Fremington, Stokenham and the hds. of Cliston, Axminster and Colyton [371/1](11). Constables' names only. Latin.

**County** [E.199/9/35]. Fairly extensive return giving arrears of persons by hundreds and parishes.

**Devon**: P.R.O., continued

*Subsidies*

**1663. North Tawton, Witheridge** [102/489] (350). First m. badly faded and largely illegible, remainder legible.
**Same hds.** [102/523](500). Parts badly decayed or faded, but parts adequate condition and legibility.
**Black Torrington hd.** [102/543](40). Repaired, but some decay, poor legibility.
**Shebbear, Hartland hds.** [245/15](500). Repaired. Some loss from decay.
**Halbarton, Hayridge, Tiverton, Bampton hds.** [102/517](250). Some decay, repaired. Part adequately legible, but much faded or decayed; **same hds.**, plus **Hemyock** [102/524](1,000).
**Lifton hd.** [102/521](60). Repaired but much lost through decay; legibility variable.
**Stanborough hd.** [102/522](250). VG.
**Plympton, Ermington hds.** [245/16](400).

*Poll Tax*

*Note*. Dr Tom Arkell, who has made a special study of the Poll Tax, considers that some or all of these may not be Poll Tax records. The Devon section of the P.R.O. calendar has been revised in modern times, and they are described as such in that.

**1660. Axminster, Colyton hds.** [245/14/4] (2,300). Repaired. Great loss from decay.
**Exeter** city [102/482]. Published in *Exeter in the Seventeenth Century*. St Mary de Grad (140) has been discovered since publication. Defaulters [102/554](300), paper, in good condition, good legibility.
**Exminster hd.** [245/14/3](4,000). Paper book, repaired: Bishopsteignton [272/48](200), paper, poor condition; Dawlish [272/45](60), paper, repaired; Ide [272/47](100), paper; Kenn [272/43] (250), poor condition. Mamhead [272/46] (75); Powderham [369/22](100), poor condition, variable legibility; West Teignmouth [272/42](300), repaired; certificiates of defaulters [102/555] (50), repaired, bound as book, easy to use but few names.
**Plympton hd.** [102/481](1,500), repaired but some decay, legibility variable.
**Wonford hd.** [245/14/1](1,000). Repaired, considerable loss from decay. [245/14/2](4,000). Paper book, repaired, great loss from decay. Incl. Dunsford, Wonford St Thomas the Apostle, Topsham,

**Devon**: P.R.O., *Poll Tax*, contd.

Whitstone; pauper East Quarter Exeter; Tedburn St Mary [102/518b](250), paper book, lower half decayed and missing, but excellent in surviving part - listing all inhabitants over 16. Upton Pyne [272/39]. Unfit for production. Defaulters (also **Wonford West hd**)[102/552](?50). Paper. well repaired, bound as book, easy to use but few names.

***Association Oath Rolls*, 1695** [C.213]

[68-71] **County**; [72-74] **Exeter**;
[75] **Totnes**; [76-78] **Plymouth**;
[79] **Okehampton**; [80] **Barnstaple**;
[81] **Plympton**; [82] **Honiton**;
[83] **Ashburton**; [84] **Dartmouth**;
[85] **'Beralston'** (? Belstone);
[86] **Tiverton**; [87] **Great Torrington**;
[88] **Crediton**; [89] **Bideford**;
[90] **Ottery St Mary**; [91] **South Molton**;
[92] **Topsham.**

Devon Record Office, Castle Street, Exeter EX4 3PQ.

*Hearth Tax*

**1662M.** Constables' original lists for **Crediton hd.**: Colebrook, Crediton, Kennerleigh, Morchard Bishop, Sandford; **Exminster hd.**: Ashcombe, Ashton, Chudleigh, Dawlish, Diddiscombe, Dunchideock, Exminster, Ide, Kenn, Mamhead, Powderham, Shillingford, East and West Teignmouth; **Plympton hd**: Brixton, Plymstock, Revelstoke, Shaugh, Wembury, Yealmpton; **Stanborough hd.**: West Alvington, Buckfastleigh, Churchstow, Dean Prior, Holne, North Huish, Moreleigh, Rattery; **Tavistock hd.**: Brentor, Milton Abbot, Tavistock.
**Exeter** city muniments: **1671M, 1672M, 1673L, 1674L.** The first is published in *Exeter in the Seventeenth Century*.

***Association Oath Roll, 1696***
**County** [Devon Q/S20/1].

Westcountry Studies Library, Exeter Central Library, Castle Street, Exeter.

Microfilm of all P.R.O. *Hearth Tax* holdings listed above.
Transcript of *Hearth Tax* **1671-74**, for **Exeter**, as in City Muniments, in collection of Devon and Cornwall Record Society (temporary membership available on the spot).

British Library (Dept. of Manuscripts)

*Marriage Act*, **1698**: Buckfastleigh, Ringmore [BM.HAIL.6832].

## Dorset

Publication

*Hearth Tax*, **1664M**, in *Dorset Hearth Tax Assessments 1662-64* [Bodleian Lib., Oxford, Rawlinson MSS. B.292-296], pub. Dorset Natural Hist. & Arch. Soc., 1951. **County** for **1664M** (11,500 names) based on and little different from 1662M. Excludes county borough of Poole. Indexed. Introduction by C.A.F. Meekings describes P.R.O. documents.

Public Record Office [E.179]

***Hearth Tax*** *(Assessments and returns)*

**1663M/1664L. County** [245/25]. Constables' returns, paper, bound into 3 books of 272ff (too much variation to estimate number of names). Includes exempt.
**1673L. County** [105/342a]( ? ). Badly decayed and most names lost, though numbers of hearths survive. Analysed in published volume, above, Appx. 7.
**1673. Poole** [245/26](?100). Badly decayed, repaired, but little legible.
**1674L. County** [105/346]( ? ). Much decayed though repaired. Faded and mainly illegible.
*(Exemption certificates)*
**1671-74** [327/1](many). Unarranged ptd. forms, no obvious order.

***Poll Tax*** (?)
**1661-2. Poole** [245/24](450). Paper; variable legibility. Arranged alphabetically (initial letter) by landlord; tenants and some streets given.

***Benevolence Money*** *(Free & Voluntary Gift?)*
**(1661?).** Sutton Waldron [245/23](24). Paper.

***Association Oath Rolls*, 1695** [C.213]
[93-94] **County**; [95-96] **Poole**;
[97] **Dorchester**; [98] **Lyme Regis**;
[99] **Weymouth**; [100] **Bridport**;
[101] **Shaftesbury** [102] **Wareham**;
[103] **Corfe Castle**; [104] **Bere Regis**.

Bodleian Library, Oxford

***Hearth Tax*** *(Assessment)*
**1664M. County** [Rawlinson MSS. B.292-96] (11,500). Published. [Dorchester, B.293; Shaftesbury, B.296; Sherborne, B.292; Blandford, B.294; Bridport, B.295].

Dorset Record Office,
County Hall, Dorchester DT1 1XJ.

***Marriage Tax***
**Lyme Regis**, 1695, 1698-9, 1701-3 [B.7/H2].
**Colway** tithing, c.1695 [B.7/H2].

## Co. Durham

Publication

'The Hearth Tax', *J.Nhumbd. & Durham FHS*, **3**, 3 (Aug 1978), pp.88-89, gives details of Northumberland and Durham records at the P.R.O. and elsewhere.

Public Record Office [E.179]
(asterisked items are also on microfilm at the Durham County Record Office)

***Hearth Tax*** *(Assessments and returns)*

**1662M. County** [106/20](1,200).
**1663L. County** [106/21]*(1,200).
**1664L. County** [106/27]*(8,000). Parts decayed or faded, but mostly legible.
**1665M. County** [245/27]*(7,500). Exempt not shown. Includes Bedlingtonshire, Norhamshire and Holy Island.
**1666L. County** [106/28]*(16,000). VG, paper ms., stitched at top, flat, easy to use. Contents list of wards. Incl. Bedlingtonshire, Norhamshire and Holy Island.
**1670M. County** [106/26](?1,000). Poor condition, repaired, and legibility. Introduction and contents list.
**1671M? County** [375/5]*(250). Variations since 1670M. Includes Bedlingtonshire, Norhamshire and Holy island.
**1674L. County** [106/25]*(14,000). Incl. Bedlingtonshire, Norhamshire and Holy Island.
**(? yr). Durham** [244/38](12). Fragment, Chester ward, west divn. of Whickham.
**Durham** [245/28](100). Bad legibility. Not clear if Hearth Tax at all.
*(Arrears)*
**1662M. County** [106/22]*(2,000). Desperate.
**1662M-1663L. County** [106/23]*(500).
**1666L. County** [106/24]*(1,250). Flat parchment sheets. Includes Bedlingtonshire, Norhamshire and Holy Island.

***Association Oath Rolls*, 1695** [C.213]
[105] **County**; [106] **Durham** city.

Durham County Record Office,
County Hall, Durham DH1 5UL.

Microfilm of P.R.O. held *Hearth Tax* records asterisked above.

## Essex

Publication

Analysis of *Hearth Tax* returns for **Ongar hd.**, *V.C.H. Essex*, vol.4, 1956, pp.303-10, by K.H. Burley.

Index

*Hearth Tax*, **1662M** [Essex Record Office Q/RTh 1](20,000). For all parishes; poor persons excluded.

Public Record Office [E.179]

***Free and Voluntary Present*, 1661-2**
**County** [246/7](3,000). Occupations given.

***Hearth Tax*** *(Assessments and returns)* (Microfilm copies of HT rolls 1662-75 are in Essex Record Office [T/A 169])

**1662M. County** [246/8](5,000). Badly decayed but repaired. Much lost from decay and surviving ms. often faded.
**Barking** and **Woodham Ferris** [246/9] (250). Paper.
**Danbury** [246/10](70). Paper, poor condition.
**Margaretting, Liston** (exempt), **H--ing** [358]. Constables' stray returns.
**1664M. Dengie hd.** [246/25](2,000). Paper book, annotated. VG.
**Freshwell hd.** [246/14](600). Annotated paper book. VG.
**Hinckford hd.** [112/687](2,400). Paper book, annotated. VG.
**Hinckford hd.** [246/26](2,500). Paper book. VG.
**Uttlesford** and **Clavering hds.** [246/13] (4,000). Annotated paper book, VG.
**Uttlesford** and **Clavering hds.** [246/28] (1,500). Paper book, VG.
**Uttlesford, Freshwell** and **Clavering hds.** [246/27](2,250). Paper book, VG.
**1665L. Uttlesford, Freshwell** and **Clavering hds.** [246/17](2,500). Annotated paper book, VG.
**1665M. Uttlesford, Freshwell, Clavering hds.** [246/16](2,000); **Winstree hd.** [246/18](1,000). Annotated paper books.
**(1665). Lexden hd.** [246/15](4,000). Paper book, annotated. VG.
**1666L. Becontree hd.** [246/24](1,200). Annotated paper book. VG.
**1666M. Uttlesford, Freshwell, Dunmow, Tendring, Hinckford, Winstree, Lexden hds.** and **Colchester** [246/20](10,000). Annotated paper book, VG.
**(1666). Harlow, Waltham, Witham, Chelmsford, Clavering, Chafford, Barstable, Ongar, Havering hds.** [246/19] (9,000). Annotated paper book, VG.



**(1667). Rochford hd.** [246/21](2,000). Annotated paper book, VG.
**(1673). County** [246/12](5,000). Badly decayed but repaired. Much lost from decay, but legible when surviving.
**(1675). County** [246/22](12,000).
**(? yr).** Haverhill and Wethersfield [246/29](150).

***Subsidies***
**1663. Barstable** and **Chafford hds.** [112/694](400).
**Chelmsford hd.** [112/695](300).
**Colchester** [112/692]. Badly decayed.
**Dengie hd.** [112/693](93). Flat sheets.
**Ongar hd.** [112/696](100). Badly torn, faded but legible.
**Uttlesford** and **Clavering hds.** [112/691] (400). Most legible, parts badly worn.
**(1664). Ongar, Harlow, Waltham** [112/697] (?300). Very badly decayed, repaired. Legibility adequate when not lost.
**Uttlesford** and **Clavering hds.** [112/615a] (100). Much lost from decay, repaired.
**(? yr).** Barfield Saling and Magna, some other places [246/29](500).

***Association Oath Rolls*, 1695** [C.213]
[107] **County**; [108] **Colchester**;
[473] **Colchester** Quakers;
[109-10] **Maldon**; [111] **Saffron Walden**;
[112] **Harwich**.

Essex Record Office,
County Hall, Chelmsford CM1 1LX.

All *Hearth Tax* holdings of the P.R.O. are on microfilm at E.R.O. [T/A 169].
There is an Index to the 1662M Hearth Tax [E.R.O. Q/RTh 1](20,000) for all parishes, poor persons excluded.

***Hearth Tax*** (see *Guide to the E.R.O.*, F.G. Emmison, 1969, page 29)

**1662M. County** [Q/RTh 1](20,000). Enrolment of returns. Complete for every parish and constablewick; excludes exempt poor. **Indexed.**
**1668.** [Q/RTh 2]. Poor persons and householders having an increase or decrease in hearths since 1663. Orig. returns by constables and collectors. 1 bundle for Hds. of Chelmsford, Clavering, Dunmow, Freshwell, Hinckford, Lexden, Tendring and Uttlesford, and liberty of Havering and town of Colchester.
[Q/RTh 3-4]. Enrolment of returns of increases and decreases in hearths since ?1663. Two rolls. Same Hds. as in Q/RTh 2.

**Essex**: Essex R.O., *Hearth Tax*, contd.

**1671L. County** [Q/RTh 5](25,000). Enrolment. Complete. Incl. exempt, and number of poor receiving alms, un-named.
**1672** (July). **County** [Q/RTh 6]. Original returns of increases and decreases in hearths. Complete. Also includes new householders.
**County** [Q/RTh 7]. Enrolment of Q/RTh 6.
**1673M.** [Q/RTh 8]. Copies of returns (15 booklets); complete except for Hds. of Barstable, Becontree (part), Chafford, Clavering, Harlow and Liberty of Havering. Includes exempt poor.
**(c.1673).** [Q/RTh 9]. Copies of returns. (7 booklets). Incomplete; for Hds. of Becontree, Clavering, Dunmow, Lexden, Tendring and Witham, liberty of Havering and town of Colchester. Names differ only slightly from same Hds. in Q/RTh 8. This may be a fair copy.
**Newport** parish book [D/P 15/8/1] incl. lists of hearths 1662, 1663; and exemptions 1668, 1671.
**Wormingford** register [D/P 185/1/1] incl. list of persons exempt from HT 1668.

***Subsidies***
**1663, 1664. Becontree Half hd.** [D/DCv 1, ff.4-5,7-8].

***(Royal) Aid***
**1664-5. Becontree** and **Havering** [D/DMs 023/1-21; D/DMy 15M50/670,671].
**1689. Havering Liberty** [D/DMs 025/1-4].
**1664-1704. Newport** parish book [D/P 15/8/1].

***Poll Tax***
**1690. Great Dunmow**: Bigods Quarter [D/DB 1112].
**Newport** parish book [D/P 15/8/1].

***Land Tax***
**1698. Becontree, Chafford, Havering** [D/DMs 027/1-28].

***Marriage Tax***
Little Parndon, 1695, 1697, 1699 [D/P 34/1/2].

***Window Tax***
**Maldon** borough [D/B 3/3/412].

***Other assessments, rates, etc.***
**Great Dunmow**: Bigod's Quarter, monthly assessment, 1669 [D/DB 1109]; assessment, 1671 [D/DB 1110]; tax for disbanding the army 1679/80 [D/DB 1111].
**Little Sampford**: vestry book incl. tax assessments, 1667-1704 [D/P 122/8/1].
**Writtle**: rate, 1667 [D/DP 07/6].

## Gloucestershire and Bristol

Publications

'The Hearth Tax in Bristol' and 'Bristol Tax Assessments in the Later Stuart Period (1660-1715)', both by J.S.W. Gibson, *Jnl. of Bristol & Avon FHS*, **36, 37,** describes the various tax lists in the Bristol Record Office.

*The Inhabitants of* ***Bristol*** *in* ***1696***, Elizabeth Ralph and Mary Williams, Bristol Record Soc., vol.25, 1968, from the Tax on marriages, births and burials, bachelors and widowers. The original records, complete for all 18 Bristol parishes, are in the Bristol Record Office (12,800 names). Indexed.

*Hearth Tax*: **Olveston** (Glos.), **1671** [from G.R.O. photocopy](60), incl. Upper Tockington, *Jnl. of Bristol and Avon FHS*, **26** (Winter 1981).

Public Record Office [E.179]

***Hearth Tax*** *(Assessments and returns)*

**1662M. County** [116/554](7,500). Fair copy. Part entirely lost, part repaired, reasonable condition and legibility. Introduction and contents list of hds.
**Bristol** [247/11](1,600). In Latin. Parchment sheets, some decay, but repaired. Good when not decayed.
**1664L. County** [247/16](?15-20,000). Detailed contents list with each hd. in separate bound sections. Much decay and poor legibility. Introductions give number of hearths.
**Bristol** [375/16](600). Very badly decayed and much also illegible from fading. Short ms., repaired and sewn at top. Detailed introduction.
**1671L. Bristol** [116/541](3,000). Includes exempt poor.
**1671L-1672L. County** [247/13](15-20,000). Badly decayed, repaired. Mostly good legibility when not lost from decay. Introduction and contents list of hds.
**1672M. County** [247/14](20,000). Decayed and faded in parts, but much OK. Introduction and contents of hds. (2 vol. photostat copy at Glos. R.O.)
**1673L. Bristol** [247/15](?3,000). Very badly decayed. Ms. stitched head to foot. Not much examined, but mostly illegible. Modern contents list and introduction; similar to **1671L** 116/541.
*(Exemption certificates)*
**1672-3. County** [116/544](5,000). Loose paper sheets, easy to use.
*(Arrears - hopeful)*
**1663L. Gloucester** (city)[116/539](200).

**Gloucestershire & Bristol**: P.R.O., ctd.

*Subsidies*

**1663. Berkeley, Grumboldsash, Langley and Swineshead, Thornbury, Henbury, Pucklechurch** and **Barton Regis hds.** [247/12](1,000).

**Forest of Dean** (divn.)[116/538](110). Poor condition.

**Bristol** [116/537](200). Bad condition and mostly illegible.

**(?1663). Bristol** [116/547](100). Poor condition, part badly faded.

*Poll Tax*

**(1660). Kiftsgate** (upper divn.) [116/535](500). Very badly decayed, but much remains legible.

***Association Oath Rolls*, 1695** [C.213]
[113] **County**; [114] **Gloucester**;
[115] **Cirencester**; [116] **Tewkesbury**;
[117] **Tetbury**; [223-24] **Bristol.**

Gloucestershire Record Office, Worcester Street, Gloucester GL1 3DW.
(Daily charge made.)

*Hearth Tax*

**1672M. County** [D.383]. 2 vol. photostat copy of P.R.O. E.179/247/14.

**1662M** and **1671-2. Kemerton** [D4614/16]. Photocopies of P.R.O. E.179/116/554 and E.179/247/14.

**1662. Alderley** [D1086/R2]. Constables' book. Original return of hearths assessed for poor rate.

**1674. Cirencester St John Baptist** [P86a CW2/1]. Churchwardens' accounts: List of persons exempt.

**1686. Westbury-on-Severn** [P354 CO 1/2].

*Subsidies, Aids, etc.*

**Westbury-on-Severn** [P354 CO 1/2]: 1664/5; 1666; 1668; 1671; 1677; 1692/3.

**Swindon**, 1677 [D 2375/X1].

*Land Tax*

**Shipton Moyne**, 1700 [D1571/E304].
**Stinchcombe**, 1710, 1722 [P312 MI/1].
**Woolaston**, 1710 [D2700/14209].
**Tidenham**, 1714 [D2700/14203].

*Window Tax*

**Stinchcombe**, 1710 [P312 MI/4].

Gloucester City Library.

**Painswick.** *Hearth Tax*, **1672L** [9930]. Certificate of persons exempt.

Warwickshire Record Office, Warwick.

**Welford on Avon.** *Marriage Tax*, c.**1695**, in constables' book.

Bristol Record Office, The Council House, College Green, Bristol BS1 5TR.

See *Guide to the Bristol Archives Office*, E. Ralph, 1971, pp.45-48.

This Office has a magnificent collection of tax assessments from 1663 on, comparable only with the City of London. Rather than separate them into different tax categories, they are shown in chronological order of assessment, following approximately the order of the published *Guide*. However, they are so numerous that it is not practicable to indicate the number of documents for each tax, their references nor the number of names each may include.

**1663-4.** Subsidy.
**1665-8.** Aid.
**1665-73.** Hearth Tax. **1671 indexed.**
**1666-7.** Poll Tax, maintenance of war.
**1667-8.** Additional Aid.
**1671.** Subsidy, supply of extraordinary occasions.
**1673-4.** Supply of extraordinary occasions.
**1677-8.** Thirty ships of war.
**1678.** Poll Tax, war with France.
**1679-80.** Supply for disbanding the army.
**1679-80.** Further supply for disbanding the army.
**1689.** Aid.
**1689.** Poll Tax, reduction of Ireland.
**1689.** Aid, defence of the realm.
**1689-90.** Aid.
**1689-90.** Poll and Additional Poll Tax for reduction of Ireland.
**1690.** Poll Tax, reduction of Ireland and war with France.
**1691-3.** Aid (Land Tax), war with France.
**1692-3.** Poll Tax, war with France.
**1693-5.** Aid, war with France.
**1694-5.** Poll Tax, war with France.
**1696-1706.** Tax on marriages, births and burials, bachelors and widowers, war against France. 1696 (complete for the 18 parishes) published, see above.
**1696-1707.** Aid, war with France.
**1696.** Several rates on houses, etc.
**1699-1814.** Several rates or duties on houses; Houses, Windows and Lights Tax.
**1698-9.** Disbanding the forces.
**1698.** Quarterly Poll Tax.
**1699.** Disbanding the army.
**1701.** Defraying expenses of Navy, Guards and Garrisons.
**1702-1849.** Aid and Land Tax.
**1703.** Subsidies, war against France and Spain.
**1696-1798.** Land Tax.

## Hampshire

Published

*Hearth Tax Returns for the Isle of Wight, **1664** to **1674***, ed. P.D.D. Russell. Isle of Wight County Record Office, 1981. Indexed. This includes **all** HT records relating to the Isle of Wight from the various P.R.O. E.179 documents listed below. Very detailed introduction with description of all records. Appendix lists Isle of Wight arrears 1669-73.

Public Record Office [E.179]

***Free and Voluntary Present*, 1661-2**
**County** [176/559](?4,000). Parchment roll, ms. stitched head to foot. Very long and unwieldy, good condn. and leg. Ts transcript of IoW at IoW R.O.
**Southampton** [176/571](150). Bad condn.

***Hearth Tax*** *(Assessments and returns)*
(IoW records published; photocopies of Winchester lists in Hampshire R.O.)

**1664L. County** [375/32](17,700). Basingstoke, Kingsclere, Isle of Wight and Alton divns., some losses; Fawley and New Forest divns., considerable losses; Andover and Portsdown divns., little remains.
**1664** March/June. **County** [176/564](6,000). Miscellaneous paper returns, bound. Introduction and contents list. Easy to use, though poor handwriting.
**1665L. County** [176/565](20,000). Shows exempt poor. New Forest annotated, increases and decreases. Microfilm at Hampshire Record Office.
**1670M. Southampton** [247/29](500). Flattened parchment sheets, easy to use.
**1673L. County** [176/569](20,000). Repaired but some loss from decay to lower parts of ms.
**1674L. County** [247/30](24,000). Poor condition and faded, but better than 176/569. Contents list of parishes.
*(Exemption certificates)*
**1670-1. County** [176/568](5,000). Paper, mainly printed, bound in two books.
**1673-4. County** [176/570](4,000). Loose folded paper sheets, no special order.
*(Arrears)*
See Isle of Wight published volume.

***Subsidies***
**1663** May. **Alton, Selborne, East Meon, Finchdean, Bishops Sutton hds** [247/26] (450). Marked 'unfit for production' but in fact in adequate preservation.
**1663** Oct. Same hds. [175/540](400).



**1663** Nov. **Fawley hd.** [176/560](65). Bad condition.
**(1663). Fawley, Buddlesgate, Mansbridge, Mainsborough, Bountisford hds.** [176/563] (500). Bad condition and legibility.
**1663/4** Mch. **Kingsclere, Evingar, Pastrow, Overton, Chuteley hds.** [176/561](400).
**Portsdown divn, Bosmere, Fareham, Titchfield, Hambledon, Bishops Waltham hds, Havant liberty** [247/28](500).
**(1664). Basingstoke, Bermondspit, Mitcheldever, Odiham, Crondall, Holdsholt hds., Bentley liberty** [247/27](500). Repaired. Some loss from decay.
**Isle of Wight** [176/562](200).
**No date. Portsdown** [176/581](150). Bad fading and staining in part.
**Barton Stacey hd.** [176/583](60). Bad condition. Incl. Nuton Stacey, Sutton Scotney, Priors Dean and Colmere, Headbourne Worthy.

***Poll Tax***
**(1660). Evingar, Kingsclere hds.** [176/558](500). Very bad condition.

***Association Oath Rolls*, 1696** [C.213]
[240] **County** (incl. Winchester);
[241] **Southampton;** [242-3] **Portsmouth;**
[244] **Portsmouth Dockyard;**
[245] **Yarmouth;** [246] **Petersfield;**
[247] **Newport;** [248] **Stockbridge;**
[249] **Christchurch;** [250] **Lymington;**
[251] **Whitchurch;** [252] **Andover;**
[253] **Basingstoke;** [254] **Romsey;**
[255] **Gosport;** [256] **Isle of Wight.**

Hampshire Record Office, 20 Southgate Street, Winchester SO23 9EF.

***Hearth Tax***
**1665L. County** [microfilm of P.R.O. E.179/176/565].
Photocopies of **Winchester** P.R.O. E.179:
**1664.** The City, The Soke and Milland [176/564].
**1665L.** The City, The Soke, Milland, Alton, Fawley, Chilcombe, Avington, Sparkford and Weeke [176/565].
**1670.** Exemption certificates [176/568].
**1673.** The City, The Soke, St Peter Chesil, Avington, Chilcombe, Weeke, Winnall, Sparkford (parts)(also exemption certificates)[176/569,570].
**1674.** The City, The Soke, St Maurice, St John, St Peter Chesil [247/30].
*also*
**1663.** Michelmersh [from Dorset Hearth Tax Returns: Photocopy 69].

**Hampshire**: Hampshire Record Office, ctd.

*Poll Tax*

**1689.** Hurn and Parley [7M54/264].
**1699.** East Woodhay [Photocopy 362 of original in Berkshire Record Office].

***Miscellaneous***

Hurn and Parley (premises in). Receipt book of Edward Hooper for payments for Hearth Tax, Window Tax, Land Tax, Royal Aids, Subsidies, parish rates, etc., 1664-78, 1701-50, 1753-5 [7M54/264].
Hurn and East Parley, Royal Aid, 1665, 1691 [7M54/262].

***Window Tax***

**1714.** Headbourne Worthy [27M60/L11].

***Land Tax***

Binsted. 1689, 1691-3, 1698, 1701, 1704, 1710 [3M51/537-543].
West Boarhunt. 1703, 1704, 1715 [5M50/1254-1261].
Portchester. 1707 [5M50/1420].
Southwick. 1710, 1712, 1715 [5M50/1848-1850].
Wymering. 1704, 1705, 1712 [5M50/1949-1952].

Southampton Civic Record Office, Civic Centre, Southampton SO9 4XL.

***Free and Voluntary Present*, 1661-2**

**Southampton,** all wards [SC/14/2/32a].

***Hearth Tax***

**1662M.** All wards [SC/14/2/32b].

***Assessments for Aids and Subsidies***

[all refs. preceded by SC/14/2/]
**1664-5, 1668, 1674; 1689; 1691; 1692:** All wards [33-6; 39-42a; 43-4; 45-7].
**1693.** St Lawrence [54].
**1694; 1697-8:** All wards [55-61; 83-8,97]
**1699.** All wards except Holy Rood [98-103].

***Poll Tax*** [all refs. SC/14/2/]

c.**1678.** All Saints [37b].
**1678.** St John (incomplete)[38].
**1689.** Holy Rood [42b].
**1692; 1697:** All wards [48-54; 89-94].
**1698.** All Saints Infra and Extra [95-96].
**1699.** All wards except St Mary [104-10].

***Marriage Tax***

**1695-97.** All parishes (some incomplete for 1695)[SC/14/2/62a-82b]. Indexed.

Isle of Wight Record Office, 26 Hillside, Newport, Isle of Wight PO30 2EB.

Ts transcript of IoW portion of *Free and Voluntary Present 1661*, by P. Russell [P.R.O. E.179/176/559].

## Herefordshire

Publications

'The *Hearth Tax* in Herefordshire', by M.A. Faraday, *Transactions of the Woolhope Naturalists' Field Club, Herefs.*, vol.41, 1973, Pt.1, pp.77-90. Returns described and compared, but no names, statistical table of totals only. Totals for 1662M, 1664L, 1664M, 1666L, 1671M below taken from this article.

'The *Hearth Tax*', by John Harnden, *Herefs FHS Jnl* **2** 8 (Winter 85) pp.335-8.

Public Record Office [E.179]

***Free and Voluntary Present*, 1661-2**

**County** [248/11](3,000). Rolls, badly decayed at foot, repaired and flattened. Parts illegible through decay, otherwise in good legible condition.

***Hearth Tax*** *(Assessments and returns)*

**1662M. County** [119/482](8,092). Poor legibility on earlier ms. but OK for most.
**1664L. County** [119/492](13,008). Exempt poor included. Mf and trs. at H.R.O.
**1664M. County** [119/485/4](7,803).
**1665L. County** [119/485/3](7,600). Annotated.
**1665M. County** [119/486](7,600). VG. Annotated. Microfilm and indexed TS transcript at Hereford Record Office.
**1666L. County** [119/487](?9,000). VG.
**1670M. County** [248/13](?14,000). Repaired but some loss from decay and much poor legibility, though some ms. are OK.
**1671M. County** [248/14](13,789). First few ms. illegible from staining or fading, but most OK. Exempt poor incl.
**1673L. County** [119/493](7,800). Brief contents list by CAFM. Missing 1m. (Greytree hd.). Some decay, repaired, much faded and illegible, parts OK.

*Note.* Of these, Faraday states those for 1664L, 1665L and 1671M are best.

*(Exemption certificates)*

**1662-1674** [331](very many). Two boxes.
1. Flat, paper certificates.
2. Bag, with paper certs. in rolls, some ptd. Also incl. Herts. and Hunts.

*(Arrears)*

**1671. County** [358].

***Subsidies***

**1662/3. Radlow hd.** [248/12](150).
**Wigmore hd.** [119/484](211). 4ms., sewn head to foot.
**(1664). Wigmore hd.** [237/45](227).

**Herefordshire**: P.R.O., continued

***Poll Tax***

**1678. County** [119/491](?300). Collectors' names only, except for short lists of defaulters for Leominster and Lydley.

**Leominster** [237/46](300). Paper. VG. Arranged by ward. Transcript at H.R.O.

***Association Oath Rolls*, 1695** [C.213]
[118] **County;** [119] **Hereford;**
[120] **Leominster.**

County Record Office (Hereford and Worcester C.C.), The Old Barracks, Harold Street, Hereford HR1 2QX.

Mfs of *Hearth Tax* **1664L** and **1665M, County** [P.R.O. E/179/119/492 & 486]. Indexed TS transcripts (also at S of G).

Transcript of *Army Disbandment Tax*, **1678, Leominster** [P.R.O. E.179/237/46], by Michael Faraday.

## Hertfordshire

Public Record Office [E.179]

***Hearth Tax*** *(Assessments and returns)* (microfilm copies at Hertfordshire R.O.)

**1662M. County** [375/30](?5,500). Introduction and parish contents list by CAFM. Very variable, some excellent.

**1663L. County** [248/23](many). Constables' returns. Loose paper sheets, repaired, in no special order. Contents list.

**1663M. County** [248/24](many). Constables' returns. Cashio hd. missing. Paper sheets, arranged by hd., repaired and guarded. Introduction by CAFM.

**1664M-1665M. Braughin hd.** [248/27](1,400). Paper book. Some pp. torn, but usable.

**1666L.** Sub-collectors' sworn statements. Paper lists for Cheshunt, Rickmansworth, Sarratt, Abbots Langley, Hemel Hempstead, Tring, Freisden, Northchurch, Gt Gaddesden, Watford, Cashio, Oxhey only [248/25](350).

**Hertford** and **Braughin hds.** [248/28] (850). Collector's paper book. VG.

**(1666L). Hertford hd.** [248/28](150). Collector's paper book. Includes St John's Wormeley, St Margaret's Amwell. Shows exempt poor, etc.

**1670. Hitchin** [121/349](245). Paper, schedule of exemptions, by ward.

**1673L. County** [375/31](?9,000). Introduction and contents list of parishes by CAFM. Much decay, repaired. Legibility generally poor.

*(Exemption certificates)*

**1670–74.** [331]. As entry under Herefs.

**Hertfordshire**: P.R.O., continued

***Subsidies***

**1663. Cashio hd.** [121/346](500).

**No date. Broadwater, Hitchen hds.** [121/353](137). Torn at foot.

***Association Oath Rolls*, 1695** [C.213]
[121] **County;** [122] Lord Lieutenant, etc.
[123-24] **St Albans;** [125] **Hertford.**

Hertfordshire Record Office, County Hall, Hertford SG13 8DE.

The Herts. R.O. has microfilm of all P.R.O. *Hearth Tax* returns listed left.

***Hearth Tax***

**1662, 1663.** Essendon, list of hearths [D/P37 8A/1].

***Subsidies*** *and* ***Land Tax Assessments***

**1655–1724.** Essendon [D/P37 8A/1].

***Land Tax***

**1690. Cashio, Dacorum hds.**

From **1711.** Parishes in **Cashio, Hertford, Braughin, Broadwater hds.**

## Huntingdonshire

Public Record Office [E.179]

***Hearth Tax*** *(Assessments and returns)*

**1664L. County** [122/227](?4,000). Badly decayed and much illegible.

**1664M. County** [122/226](6,500). Annotated.

**1666L. County** [249/1](6,800). Paper book. Good.

**1670M-1673L. County** [249/4](1,000). Much lost from decay, repaired. Includes part of Hurstington hd.

**1674L. County** [249/2](6,800).

*(Exemption certificates)*

**1670–74.** [331]. As entry under Herefs.

***Association Oath Rolls*, 1695** [C.213]
[126] **Huntingdonshire;** [127] **Huntingdon;**
[128] **Godmanchester.**

County Record Office (Cambs. C.C., Huntingdon Branch), Grammar Schoool Walk, Huntingdon PE18 6LF.

Microfilm of P.R.O. *Hearth Tax* records E.179/122/226, 249/1,2,4 (also *Poll Tax* 249/3, 1692, parish totals only).

***Window Tax***

Stanground. 1698-1752 [2776/18/9-12].
Great Catworth, 1702 [DDM 5C/8].

## Kent

Publications

*Kent Hearth Tax Enrolled Assessment **1664L** Lathe of St Augustine* (eastern half of county) [Kent Archives Office Q/RTh] (3,300), ed. D.W. Harrington, Kent FHS Record Pubn. No.14, 1983. Indexed. The Lathe of Shepway (Romney Marsh) and the remainder of the county may eventually be published.

*Sevenoaks Wills and Inventories in the Reign of Charles II*, Kent Record Soc. **25** (1988) incl. **1664L** Hearth Tax for Sevenoaks and Liberty of Riverhead.

*Hearth Tax Returns **1664**. Gravesend, Milton, Northfleet, Southfleet.* 8pp. 65p from E.R. Green, 49 Dennis Rd, Gravesend.

*Hearth Tax for the Hundred of Little and Lessness, Kent, **1662M**, **1663M*** [P.R.O. E.179/129/702/206, 179/249/31/13], extr. and indexed by J.E. Packer, 1983-85 (duplicated TS). Incl. Crayford, Erith, E Wickham, Plumstead. Copies at LB of Bexley LS Library, LB of Greenwich LH Dept, P.R.O., Soc of Gen, NW Kent FHS.

Public Record Office [E.179]

***Hearth Tax** (Assessments and returns)*

(Microfilms of Hearth Tax returns, 1662-1664 are held by Kent County Library)

For the four returns **1662M** to **1664L** there are returns for very many (perhaps all) divisions of one or more collections. That for **1662M** has over a hundred references; **1663L** has 58; **1663M** has 38; and **1664L** has 62. The calendar has been revised and retyped and is relatively easy to consult, though the order of documents and places is haphazard. The documents have not been examined and no estimate of numbers can be given.

**1671M. County, Canterbury and Cinque Ports** [129/746] (28,000). Narrow ms. Some decay, repaired, some fading, but most OK or adequate. Introduction and contents list of hds.

**1673L. County, Canterbury and Cinque Ports** [365/21] (2,000). 'Incomplete'. Considerable fading, slight decay, repaired. Introduction by CAFM.

*(Exemption certificates)*

**1674L. County, Canterbury and Cinque Ports** [129/747] (?2,500). Printed forms, repaired, bound as book.

***Subsidies***

**(1661). Maidstone and Eythorne hds.** [129/691] (200); [129/697] (200).



**(1663). Milton** [129/713] (400).
**Aylesford (lathe, south)** [129/728] (41). Maidstone, Hd. of Maidstone, Lower and Upper Half Hds. of Eythorne.

**No date. St Augustine lathe** [249/39] (250). Fragile.
**Blackheath hd.** [249/44] (100). Poor legibility.

***Poll Tax***

**No date. Shepway lathe** [129/752] (?300). Poor condition, only partly legible.
**St Augustine lathe** [129/753] (150). Names on left OK, but second column on right decayed and lost.

***Association Oath Rolls*, 1695** [C.213]
[129] **County**; [130] **Canterbury**;
[131] **Rochester**, etc; [132] **Maidstone**;
[133] **Queenborough**; [134] **Sheerness**;
[135] **Gravesend** and **Milton**;
[136] **Court of Vice-Admiralty**;
[137] **Prize Office, Dover**;
[332] **Cinque Ports**.

Kent Archives Office, County Hall, Maidstone, Kent ME14 1XQ.

***Hearth Tax***

**1664L. County** [Q/RTh] (26,000). Enrolled assessment, incl. in nearly all cases houses exempt. Omits liberties of the Cinque Ports, Romney Marsh and Canterbury. St Augustine's lathe published, Shepway lathe to be published; see above, left.

**Tenterden** borough records [Te] incl. **1663-4** HT assessment.

**New Romney** borough records [NR] incl. **1662-71** HT; and **Lydd** HT **1670**.

Darnley MSS [U1107] incl. HT assessments **1662M** for Ashford and the hds. of Aloesbridge, Bewsborough, Bleangate, Bridge and Petham, Cornilo, Eastry, Marden, Newchurch, Ringslow, Westgate and Wingham, and the borough of Longport (Canterbury).

Gordon Ward collection [U1000/10] incl. **Penshurst** HT returns **1663**.

Phillipps MSS [U1592] incl. HT returns for **Chart** and **Longbridge** hds. c.**1662M**.

***Poll Tax***

**New Romney** borough records [NR] incl. poll tax **1668-98**.

***Marriage Tax***

**1705.** 41 parishes [Q/CT] listed in *Local Population Studies*, **27, 28.**

**New Romney**, 1696, 1697, 1700 [NR].

**Wingham**, 1705, 1706 [Q/CT].

**Kent** continued

Kent County Library (Local Studies), Springfield, Maidstone, Kent ME14 2LH.

Microfilm of P.R.O. holdings of Kent *Hearth Tax*, **1662M-1664L**.

Canterbury Cathedral Archives and City Record Office, The Precincts, Canterbury.

*Hearth Tax*, **1670**, parts of Canterbury only [B/C/H/1-3].

## Lancashire

Published

*Transactions of the Historic Society of Lancashire and Cheshire*, vol.52, N.S., 16 (for 1900, pubd. 1902), pp.127-38, has an extract from the *Hearth Tax* **1662M** [P.R.O. E.179/250/6] for the **Hd. of West Derby** of all names of those possessing houses with more than three hearths (195); and, from **1673M** [P.R.O. E.179/132/355] of (apparently) **all** names for **Liverpool** (252)(probably excluding exempt poor).

**Liverpool** *Hearth Tax* **1663**[P.R.O.E.179/250/8] in *Liverpool in King Charles II's Time*, by Sir Edward Moore (1667-8), ed. W.F. Irvine, 1899, Appx. pp.167-70.

*Taxation in Salford Hundred, 1524-1802*, by J. Tait, Chetham Soc., N.S., vol.83, 1924, pp.84-119 includes extracts from *Hearth Tax* **1666L** [P.R.O. E.179/250/9] and missing places from **1664L** [E.179/250/11], but **note** only householders with three or more hearths are abstracted.

*Lancashire Association Oath Rolls, 1696*, ed. W. Gandy, 1921 (repub. 1985 by Soc of Gen). Incl. all rolls for Lancs. [C.213/138-144]. Index to surnames.

Public Record Office [E.179]

***Free and Voluntary Present*, 1661-2**
**County** [250/5](?7,500). Two rolls, one very unwieldy.

***Hearth Tax*** *(Assessments and returns)* (microfilm copies at Lancashire R.O., except for E.179/330/3)

**1662M. West Derby hd.**(part)[250/6] (?2,000). Constables' returns, paper, repaired and bound together.
**Salford, Blackburn, Leyland hds.**[330/3] Very badly decayed, not repaired, and mostly illegible. Incl. Salford: Withington; Blackburn hd.: Pendleton, Rishton; Leyland: Whittle le Woods, Charnock Richard. 'Unfit for prodn.'

**Lancashire**: P.R.O., *Hearth Tax*, contd.

**(1663). County** [250/8]. Flattened ms. 1. Salford (6,400); 2. Leyland (2,400); 3. Blackburn (3,200); 4. Lancaster (3,600); 5. Derby (6,800); 6. Lonsdale (1,600). In the Lancs. R.O. catalogue Nos. 4 and 5 are described as Amounderness and West Derby.
**1664L. County** [250/11]. Flattened ms. 1. Lonsdale (5,000); 2. Amounderness (4,000); 3. Blackburn (4,600); 4. Leyland (2,400); 5. Derby (8,200), 1m. missing (Gt & Lit Crosby, Ince Blundell, Litherland); 6. Salford (7,200); 7. County, hearths walled up (?700).
**1665M. County** [132/352]. Schedule of variations, no names.
**(1665). Leyland hd.** [132/351](2,000). Annotated. Described by Lancs. R.O. catalogue as Schedule of Variations.
**1666L. County** [250/9](?15,000). Collectors' account, paper returns, VG. Leyland, Amounderness, Lonsdale, Salford, West Derby, Blackburn.
**1671M. County** [250/13](?1,500). Schedule of variations only.
**1672M. County** [132/356](?450). Schedule of variations only.
**1673M. County** [132/355](?27,500). Lonsdale, Amounderness, Blackburn, Leyland, West Derby, Salford. Liverpool published, see left.
**(n.d.) County** [250/12](?2,000). Fragments (repaired). Good in in parts.

***Subsidies***
**(1663). Blackburn hd.** [132/350](220). Poor legibility on upper half, but OK further down.
**Lonsdale hd.** [132/348](165). Ms. sewn head to foot. Some decay at end.
[132/349](220). Ms. sewn head to foot. Some fading and staining.
[250/7](?50). Bad condn. and legibility.
**(n.d.)** [250/12,m.10]. Place unknown.

***Poll Tax***
**1660. Blackburn hd.** [250/4](?9,000). Fairly long ms., varying, sewn at top, but quite easy to use. A VG record.
**(1667). County** [250/10](300). Certificates of defaulters.
**(1677). Leyland hd.** [132/358](?350). Decayed and semi-legible at start, but much better lower down.

***Association Oath Rolls*, 1695** [C.213]
[138] **County**; [139] Duchy Court;
[140] **Lancaster**; [141] **Preston**;
[142] **Wigan**; [143] **Clitheroe**;
[144] **Liverpool**. All published.

**Lancashire**, continued

Lancashire Record Office, Preston.

***Hearth Tax***
M'film of all P.R.O. holdings listed on p.26 except for E.179/330/3.
**1664. Salford, Huncoat** and **Manchester** [QDV 14]. Original returns.
Ainsworth, Birtle, Butterworth, Castleton, Middleton, Swinton, Thornham, Urmston, Worlsey [UDV 18,19]. Exemptions.
***Poll Tax***
**1678. Bolton divn. of Salford hd.** [QDV 13].

Cumbria Record Office, Barrow.

M'film of Hearth Tax as Lancs. R.O., also Free...Present [E.179/250/5].

***Hearth Tax***
**1679M. Dalton-in-Furness** [BD/HJ 174/2].

## Leicestershire

Publication

*Hearth Tax*, **1666L** [P.R.O. E.179/251/9] in *Leicestershire Medieval Village Notes*, G.F. Farnham, 6 vols.(c.1920s), by village (alphabetical, vols.1-4, but more in vols.5-6 - see index of places, vol. 6). Some also for **1664L** [134/322, sometimes misprinted as 332], **1664M** [251/4], and **1670M** [240/279]. Not indexed.

Public Record Office [E.179]

***Free and Voluntary Present*, 1661-2**
**County** [134/317](3,000). Excellent.

***Hearth Tax*** *(Assessments and returns)*
(Microfilm copies of all references are at the Leicestershire R.O.)

**1662M. Sparkenhoe hd.** [375/18](?500). In bad condition, much illegible.
**(1664L)**(dated by Leics. R.O.). **County** [134/322](11,000).
**Leicester, East Goscote** [375/19](?250). Fragment, Beeby only place legible. In bad condition, not repaired.
**1664M. County** [251/4](12,500). Draft. Nine paper books, by hd., annotated, exempt poor shown. VG.
**County** [251/3](12,500). Enrolment of 251/4. Broad but quite short ms., easy to use. Annotated, exempt poor shown.
**1665L. County** [251/8](?12,000). Draft. Sewn paper sections. Annotated. Exempt poor shown.
**County** [251/5](?12,000). Enrolment of 251/8. Bad decay at feet of ms.

**Leicestershire**: P.R.O., *Hearth Tax*, ctd.

**1665M. County** [251/7]( ? ). Draft. Sewn paper sections. Annotated, exempt poor shown.
**County** [251/6](12,200). Enrolment of 251/7. Annotated. Exempt poor not shown.
**1666L. County** [251/9](10,500). Published. Draft, paper book. Exempt poor not shown.
**1670M. County** [240/279](11,000).
**1673L. County**, except Leicester [134/320]. 'Views of accounts'. Only alterations since 1672M listed.
*(Arrears)*
**1662M. County** [375/12]. Desperate.
**1662M-1664L. County** with Rutland [371/2]. Partly Latin. Mainly constables' names only. Many ms. faded.

***Subsidies***
**(1663). East Goscote hd.** [134/316](100). Decayed, bad condn. and legibility.
**1664. Sparkenhoe hd.** [134/315](350).
**(1664). Guthlaxton hd.** [134/318](300).

***Association Oath Rolls*, 1695** [C.213] [145] **County.**

Leicestershire Record Office,
57 New Walk, Leicester LE1 7JB.

***Hearth Tax***
All P.R.O. Hearth Tax holdings listed are on microfilm at the Leics. R.O. [MF/128-130].

*Modern transcripts*
**County, 1664L** [P.R.O. E.179/134/322], MS, by A.W. Read, indexed by parish name. Also incl. **Gartree hd., 1664M** [E.179/251/4].
**Loughborough, 1664** [E.179/134/322] (229), TS, by A.B. Clarke, 1935. Names arranged alphabetically. Also Knight Thorpe (10) and Woodthorpe (12), 1664.
**Loughborough, 1670M** [E.179/240/279] (170), alphabetical list of surnames.
**Fenny Drayton, 1670** [presumably from E.179/240/279, though incorrect ref. 133/29 is given](23). TS, with parish register transcript, by W.T. Hall.

***Poll Tax***
**Beaumanor, 1689** [DG9/2806]. Original.

***Marriage Tax***
**Leicester. St Mary, 1697-99** [BR.IV.2.6] (670); **St Martin, 1695/6** BR.IV.2.7
**St Martin, 1695/6** [BR.IV.2.7](1,200);
**St Margaret, 1699** [BR.IV.2.8](840).
**Rothley, 1695** [44'28/970/1-9].

## Lincolnshire

No published sources, but transcripts at Lincolnshire Archives Office.

Public Record Office [E.179]

***Free and Voluntary Present*, 1661-2**
**County** [140/749](7,500).

***Hearth Tax*** *(Assessments and returns)*

**(1662M). Holland** [140/805](4,000). Some decay, repaired, some loss or illegibility, but mostly OK.
**Lindsey** [140/806](3,200). About one third lost from decay, repaired. Most of surviving lists VG legibility and condition, but a few ms. badly faded.
**1662M-1664M. County** [333](many). Paper returns, unsorted.
**1665M. Holland and Kesteven** [140/754] (?18,000). In two parts. Annotated.
**1670M. Holland and Kesteven** [140/791] (10,000). Demolished hearths shown.
**1671. Lindsey** [251/14](3,500). Schedule of variations.
*(Exemption certificates)*
**1663. County**? [334](many). Unsorted, paper. Marked 'unfit for production' but in fact in good repair.
*(Arrears)*
**1662M-1663M. County** [371/3-6, 372/2-5] (450). Latin. Various sechedules of sperate, desperate and constables' arrears. Mainly constables' names.

***Subsidies***

**(1663). Holland** [140/748](600).
**Lawress, Aslacoe, Corringham, Manley wapentakes** [140/750](500);
Same, plus **Well** [140/751](650).
**Langoe wapentake** [140/752](500). Mostly in very bad condition, not repaired.
**1665. Louth, Eske, Ludborough, Calceworth** and **Hill wapentakes** [140/753](400).
**(no date). Gartree wapentake** [140/818] (?50). Faded. Very poor legibility.

***Poll Tax***

**1666-67.** Assessments: Halton Holgate [140/765](29); Pinchbeck [140/770](46). Returns of defaulters [140/756-789; 140/808-817](mostly less than ten names, but Soxhill 54).
**(no date). Candleshoe wapentake** [140/804] (1,000).

***Association Oath Rolls*, 1695** [C.213]

[146] **County**; [147] **Lincoln**;
[148] **Boston**; [149] **Great Grimsby**;
[150] **Stamford**; [151] **Grantham.**

Lincolnshire Archives Office,
The Castle, Lincoln LN1 3AB.

***Hearth Tax***

*Original:* **Lincoln** city, **1662M,** Lincoln city Quarter Sessions minute book [BROG 1/1, ff.115-124]. Also includes Waddington, Branston, Canwick and Bracebridge (then incl. in the city's jurisdiction), but there may be gaps in its coverage of the city itself.
*Transcript:* **Kesteven, 1665M** and **1670M,** TS, based on P.R.O. E.179/140/754,791. Index of places in each volume. Separate index of persons.

***Poll Tax*, 1692.** Driby, Friskney, Ingoldmells in Adlethorpe, Orby, Sutterby, Wainfleet [Lind.Dep. 35/2/1].
***Marriage Tax*. Candleshoe wapentake, 1701-03**, incomplete; **1706,** complete [Lind.Dep. 35/2/7]. At present unfit for production.

## London

Publications

*London Rate Assessments and Inhabitants' Lists in Guildhall Library and the Corporation of London Records Office*, 2nd edn. 1968 (now o.p.), gives details of almost all the relevant lists held in those two repositories - see pages 29-30, after Public Record Office entry.

*Guide to the Records at Guildhall*, P.E. Jones and R. Smith, 1951 (o.p.), pp.78-88, lists the tax assessments in C.L.R.O. (see page 29) in detail.

*London Inhabitants within the Walls*, ***1695***, introduction by D.V. Glass, London Record Society, vol.2, 1966, gives an index to 60,000 names of individuals enumerated in 80 out of 97 parishes within the City walls in connection with the Marriage Tax (see page 7).

'A Supplement to the London Inhabitants List of 1695 compiled by staff at Guildhall Library', *Guildhall Studies in London History*, **2**, 2 and 3 (Apr, Oct 1976), pp.77-104,136-57. Designed to cover the parishes missing from the Marriage Tax, listed page 30, based on 1694/5 Poll Tax and other sources.

Index (at Corporation of London R.O.) to 54,000 individuals in 13 City parishes 'without the walls' not published in the above volume. See under C.L.R.O., page 30.

**London**, continued

Public Record Office [E.179]

***Free and Voluntary Present*, 1661-2**
**London.** Arrears only [252/18](750). By ward. Paper.
**Inns of Court.** Arrears only [147/608] (11); [252/19](2).

***Hearth Tax*** *(Assessments and returns)*

**1662/3. Tower (Liberty) and St Helen (parish)** [252/26](200). Paper book.
**(1663). London** [252/27](14,000). Slight decay, repaired; opening ms. faded and decayed.
**1665M-1666L** (+ arrears). **Aldersgate, Bassishaw, Cripplegate Within and Without, St Andrew Holborn** [147/630] (4,500). Paper book, VG.
**(?1665-6). Cornhill, Lime Street, Bishopsgate, Broad Street wards** [147/617](4,000). Paper book, VG.
**Farringdon Within and Without wards** [147/627](6,500). Paper book, VG.
**1666L. London and Middlesex** [252/32] (44,000). 39 paper books, 879ff., annotated. According to CAFM, the following in the City of London are missing: **7.** St Mary Abchurch, St Martin Orgars, St Laurence Orgars, All Hallows the Great and Less; **12.** St Matthew Friday St, St John Evangelist, St Margaret Moses, St Nicholas Olave, St Mary Somerset, St Mary Mounthaw, St Nicholas Coleabbey, St Mary Magdalen Old Fish St, St Augustines; **13.** Ratcliffe, Shadwell; **14.** St Peter Cornhill, St Michael Cornhill, St Martin Outwich, St Benet Fink, St Peter le Poore, St Bartholomew Exchange, St Margaret Lothbury, St Stephen Coleman St, St Mildred Poultry, St Mary Woolchurch, St Christopher, All Hallows by the Wall; **15.** All Hallows Broad St, St Mildreds, Holy Trinity the Less, St Michael Queenhithe, St James Garlickhill, St Mary Aldermary, St Thomas Apostle, St Martin Vintry; **17.** St Annes Blackfriars, St Andrew by the Wardrobe, St Benet Pauls Wharf, St Peter Pauls Wharf; **23 & 24.** St Botolphs Bishopsgate East.
**(pre-1674). London** [147/624](10,000). Ms. sewn at top. Some decay, repaired, some fading/staining.
**(1674). London** [252/23](?20,000). Much fading.
Return of new hearths [252/24](20). Paper.
**1675. New Serjeants Inn** [252/25](16). Paper.

**London**: P.R.O., *Hearth Tax*, continued

**No date. London** [252/28](4,000). Paper book, not repaired, some pages torn and entries lost, some staining.
*(arrears)*
**1664. London** [371/7](700). Desperate.
**1670-1. London and Middlesex** [252/20] (4,000). Some fading.
**(1670-1). London** [252/21](7,000). Latin. 2ms. decayed.

***Subsidies***
**1664. Candlewick St ward** [147/609](50). Bad condition and legibility.
**Tower ward, St Dunstans in the East** [147/610](200+). Badly faded in parts.

***Poll Tax*** *(arrears, certs. of non-payment)*
**1666-7.** Bread St. [147/611](80); Tower ward [147/613](80); Lime St. [147/614] (100); Tower of London [147/615](10).
**1678.** Farringdon within, Blackfriars [147/612](75), streets named; [147/618] Incl. Coleman St.(28); Vintry (31); Aldersgate without (24); St Bartholomew the Less (4); Bassetshaw (8); Vintry, Garlickhythe (16); Farringdon without; St Bride's Middle Precinct (streets named; 150); Cripplegate within, Milk St (10); Portsoken, High St (33). [147/619](300). St Bride's precinct and Farringdon Without ward. [147/620](24). St Sepulchre parish, church precinct. [147/621](100). St Martin's le Grand. [147/623](300). St Bride's precinct.
**No date.** Portsoken, Houndsditch [252/28a] (160); [147/622](25). Holborn Cross.

***Association Oath Rolls*, 1695** [C.213] [160] Lord Mayor, Aldermen and Common Councilmen; [161-70] Various institutions of the City; [171] Guild Companies (80); [172-75] The Tower of London.

Corporation of London Records Office, PO Box 270, Guildhall, London EC2P 2EJ. (see published Guides, page 28, left)

***Hearth Tax*** *(Assessments and returns)*
c.**1670-73. City of London.** A limited number, arranged rather confusingly, partly by ward and partly by parish, but most areas are covered.

***Subsidies, Aids,*** *etc.* (see Guide, p.28)

**1661**: some wards.
**1663-4**: some wards.
**1666-8**: most wards.
**1671**: some wards.
**1673-4**: all wards.
**1677-8**: some wards.
**1680**: all wards.
**1683**: most wards.
**1688-90**: all wards.
**1693-4**: all wards.
**1696-7**: all wards.

*Poll Tax*

**1678, 1689-90, 1692-3**: almost all wards.
**1694-5, 1698**: some wards.

*Marriage Tax*

**1695**: All parishes except those listed below. Index to persons, parishes 'within the walls' published, London Record Society vol.2.

Index at CLRO to parishes outside the walls:
St Andrew Holborn (part); St Bartholomew the Great; the Less; St Botolph; without Aldersgate; Aldgate (part); and Bishopsgate; St Bride's; Bridewell precinct; St Dunstan in the West; St Giles without Cripplegate; St Olave Southwark (London Bridge precinct); St Sepulchre; Whitefriars precinct.

Parishes 'within the walls' for which records do **not** survive, and therefore not indexed in the London R.S. vol.2, but see Publications (p.28), *Guildhall Studies in London History*:
Holy Trinity the Less; St Nicholas: Acons; Cole Abbey; Olave; St Olave: Hart St.; Jewry; Silver St.; St Pancras Soper Lane; St Peter: le Poer; upon Cornhill; Westcheap; St Stephen Coleman St.; Walbrook; St Swithun London Stone; St Thoams Apostle; St Vedast Foster Lane.

British Library (Dept. of Manuscripts)

*Marriage Tax*

**1696.** St Benet and St Peter Pauls Wharf [B.M. Add.Ms.32645, ff.4-11v].

Guildhall Library (Dept. of MSS.)

*Marriage Tax*

**1704.** St Benet Sherehog [MS.7625].

## Middlesex

Publications (available in the Greater London History Library, 40 Northampton Road, London EC1R 0AB)

*Hearth Tax* for **Harrow 1674** [P.R.O. E.19/143/370] (about 300), 'The Harrow Hearth Tax', by G. Glazebrook, in *Middlesex & Hertfordshire Notes and Queries*, vol.14 (1898), pp.187-90. Indexed.

*Hearth Tax* for **Acton, 1664-1674**, transcribed by A. & T. Harper Smith, in *Acton Past & Present*, **15** (1988).



*Hearth Tax* for **Staines 1664** [G.L.R.O. MR/TH.6] (218), transcribed by H.A. Randall, in *Staines Local History Society Journal*, **6** (Feb 1972). Indexed.

*Hearth Tax* for **Ealing, Greenford, Hanwell, Northolt, Perivale, 1664L, 1666L, 1672, 1674L,** also **Ealing** only **1670M, ?1671, 1672/3**, in *Ealing in the 17th Century*, by K.J. Allison, Ealing Local History Society, Members' Paper No.4 (1963). [1666L from P.R.O. E.179/252/32; rest from G.L.R.O.].

*Poll Tax* for **Uxbridge 1693/4**, transcript of assessment for 4s. in £, from original in Corporation of London R.O., 6pp. [P.60-33 UXB].

Public Record Office [E.179]

***Free and Voluntary Present*, 1661-2**

**Westminster** [143/333] (1,600). Enrolled. No occupations. Subscriptions taken at Star Chamber, Lincolns Inn, St Martin le Grand, Covent Garden, St Clements.

***Hearth Tax*** *(Assessments and returns)*

**(1662). Ossulstone hd., Tower divn.** [253/16] (7,000).

**(1662-3). County** [253/30] (?5,000). Flattened ms. Badly decayed, not repaired, unusable at present.

**1663-4. Elthorne hd.** [253/17]. Constables' returns: Cowley (11); Harmondsworth (100); Harefield (80); Hillingdon arrears (122); Ickenham (24).

**(1664). Ossulstone hd., Holborn divn.** [143/336] (many). Very bad decay, feet of many ms. lost, repaired; legibility poor.

**Elthorne, Spelthorne and Isleworth hds.** [143/405] (2,200). Roll. Considerable decay and fading.

**1666L. County (with London).** [252/32] (44,000). 39 paper books, 879ff., annotated.

**(1674). County** [143/370] (38,500). First m. faded.

**1675. Westminster** [253/25] (9,000). By street. Fading on opening ms.

**No date. County** [253/29] (6,000). Much decay, repaired. Some loss from fading.

**County** [143/334] (?4,000). Incl. 1 good file of 31ms., other miscellaneous ms. decayed, not repaired.

**Bethnal Green** [143/390] (54). Bad condn.

**Hatton garden** [143/391] (60).

**Tower Hamlets** [143/392] (3,000). Flattened ms. Incl. 1ms. for St Giles in the Fields.

**Middlesex**: P.R.O., *Hearth Tax*, contd.

**No date. Westminster** [143/404](1,700). By ward. Repaired but much lost or faded.
**Clerkenwell**, etc. [143/406](?3,500). Repaired but badly decayed and faded.
**Tower Hamlets** [143/407](20,000). Ms. sewn at head, outer ms. damaged.
**? Westminster/Holborn** [253/28](5,000). Some decay, repaired.

*(Exemption certificates)*
**1673-5. County** [143/367](many). Paper certificates from incumbents and churchwardens. VG.

*(Arrears)*
**1664. Covent Garden**, etc. [143/335] (2,500). Paper book.
**1665M-1666L. St Andrew Holborn, St Giles in the Fields, Saffron Hill** [267](4,000). Paper book, VG.
**Gore hd.** [268](1,000). Paper book, VG.
**1670-1. County** with **London** [252/20] (4,000). Some fading.

*Subsidies*

**1660. Tower Hamlets** [143/332](1,750). VG. Strangers indicated.
**1664. Ossulstone hd., Holborn divn.** [143/337](?150). Some decay, not repaired. Much fading but parts OK.
**(1666). Westminster** [143/338](500). Certificates of defaulters.
**No date. Westminster** [143/385]( ? ). Badly decayed, some parts legible.
**Holborn** [143/393](650). Flattened ms. 2ms. badly decayed, others part decayed but otherwise OK.

*Subsidy or Aid(?)*

**1671. Tottenham** [253/21](106). By ward.
**South Mimms** [243/22](148).
**Enfield** [243/23](200).
**Edmonton** [243/24](130). By ward (date probably 1671).

*Poll Tax (Certificates of defaulters, non payment, arrears)*

*Note*. These certificates are full of evidence of mobility and of considerable interest, worthy of detailed study.

**1666. Grays Inn**, etc. [143/345](16).
**(1666). Westminster** [143/347](200).
**1667. Golden Lane**, etc. [143/346](75).
**Holborn** [143/353](250).
**Holborn (north)** [143/360](95).
**Poplar, Blackwall** [143/342](100).
**St Giles without**, Whitecross Street, etc. [143/357](100).
**St James Pall Mall** [143/354](60).

**Middlesex**: P.R.O., *Poll Tax*, *Certificates of non-payment*, *etc.*, continued

**1667. St Margaret Westminster.** Samuel Baker's ward [143/341](50); Nicholas Uphman's ward [143/355](113); [238/109] (80)(partly soldiers, absentees).
**St Martin in the Fields** [143/349](200); High Street, upper divn. of [143/352] (55); Edward Ireland's ward [143/358] (100); [253/19](28); Charing Cross [143/362](40).
**Savoy ward, Duchy of Lancaster** [252/33] (100).
**Shadwell** [143/350](150).
**East Smithfield** [143/339](250).
**Spitalfields** [143/382](100). ?1667 ("great loss by late lamentable fire").
**Wapping** [143/348](600).
**(1677). St Clement Danes** [143/401](33).
**1678. Furnivall's Inn** [143/377](28: actual taxpayers); [147/626](4).
**Grub Street** [143/378](82).
**High Holborn** [143/381](300).
**Hornsey** [143/374](25).
**Limehouse** [143/376](75).
**Minories** [143/380](20).
**St Botolph's Bishopsgate without** [143/351](136); [143/379](250).
**St Clement Danes** [143/401](33).
**St Martin in the Fields** [143/371](100).
**Savoy** [143/375](45); [143/386](35).
**Wapping** (Ratcliffe Highway) [143/373] (150); (Whitechapel) [143/372](92).
**No date. Bromley** [143/399](15).
**Chiswick** [143/394](46).
**Clerkenwell** [143/398](82).
**Hackney** [143/397](45). Incl. Church St., Mare St., Well St., Grove St.
**Hoxton** [143/402](250). **Islington** [143/396](33). **South Mimms** [143/411](13).
**Norton Folgate** [143/388](100).
**St Giles in the Fields.** Old Town divn. [143/387](25); Old Town divn. with Bloomsbury [143/403](200); Bloomsbury [143/389](250).
**St Martin in the Fields**, Drury Lane divn. [253/27](117).
**St Sepulchre Holborn** [143/400](200).
**Shoreditch** [143/383](100).
**Strand** [143/395](79).
**Whitechapel** [143/384](150).

***Marriage Tax:*** Harefield, 1699 [T.64/302].

***Association Oath Rolls*, 1695** [C.213]
[152] **County**; [153] Militia officers;
[154] Commissioners of tax;
(155: Enfield Chase - missing);
[156] **Kensington**; [157-58] **Westminster**;
[159] **St Martin le Grand.**

**Middlesex**, continued

Greater London Record Office,
40 Northampton Road, London EC1 0AB.

***Hearth Tax*** *(Assessments and returns)*

**1664.** Enrolled (parchment) copy [MR/TH: 1. Finsbury divn.; 2. Holborn divn.; 3. Brentford divn.; 4. Tower divn.; 5. Edmonton and Gore hds.; 6. Elthorne, Spelthorne and Isleworth hds.; 7. City and Liberty of Westminster]. Index to Hornsey, Finchley and Friern Barnet (all Finsbury divn.).

**1669–70.** 3½ yrs ending **1670M,** delivered 15 Apr 1672 [MR/TH.8]. Parchment engrossment. Covers most of county except Gore hd., and Westminster.

*Note*. All the other holdings are original paper returns by constables:

**1669** or earlier. **Gore hd.** [MR/TH.75].

**1670–71. Ossulstone hd.** [MR/TH.9-19]. [On microfilm M/MIC 26/1-2] Covers much of hd., environs of London.

**Spelthorne hd.** [MR/TH.20]. Also typed transcript of Hampton and Hampton Wick at G.L.R.O., open shelves, Catalogue Room, Archive Section.

**?1670–71. Edmonton hd.** [MR/TH.73-74].

**1671–72. St Giles in the Fields** [MR/TH.21].

**1672. Edmonton, Elthorne hds.** [MR/TH.22,23], paper engrossments.

Little Ealing, Old and New Brentford, Gore, Isleworth, parts of **Ossulstone hd** [MR.TH.24-38].

**1672–73. Ossulstone hd.** [MR/TH.39-42] (Acton, Chiswick, St Botolph Aldgate, St Giles in the Fields, Trinity Minories).

**1673. Ossulstone hd.** [MR/TH.43]. (Chelsea, Fulham, Kensington).

**1673/4. Ossulstone hd.** [MR/TH.44]. (St Giles without Cripplegate, St Katherine's).

**?1674. Ossulstone hd.** [MR/TH.45-48].

**Nearly all remainder of county**, except Westminster [MR/TH.49-72].

**No date. Isleworth hd.** [MR/TH.76-77].

**Ossulstone hd.** [MR/TH.78-115].

**Spelthorne hd.** [MR/TH.166-17].

*Note*. The G.L.R.O. catalogue lists the places within each hundred with the years for which returns survive.

**Middlesex**, continued

Corporation of London Records Office,
PO Box 270, Guildhall, London EC2P 2EJ.

See *London Rate Assessments and Inhabitants' Lists in Guildhall Library and C.L.R.O.*, 2nd edn., 1968 (out of print).

***Assessment for 4s. in the pound (Aid)***

**1693/4.** Most of **county** (?all).

City of Westminster Archives Department,
Victoria Library, 160 Buckingham Palace Road, London SW1W 9UD.

***Poll Tax***

**1664. St Martin in the Fields.** Return of inhabitants [F4533].

***Marriage Tax***

**1695. St Margaret's Westminster.** Collectors' books (incomplete) [E1566-69]. St Margaret's Long Ditch and Petty France wards, St Peter ward, Palace ward.

Society of Genealogists.

Hearth Tax, Isleworth 1664-1674.

## Monmouthshire

Public Record Office [E.179]

***Free and Voluntary Present*, 1661-2**
**County** [253/32](3,150). VG.

***Hearth Tax*** *(Assessments and returns)*

**1663M**(?). **County** [148/95](4,000). In Latin. Condition variable. Arrears included.

**1664L. County** [148/97](3,000). In Latin.

**No date.** Part of **County** [148/98](1,800). Flattened short parchment ms. Decayed at feet but otherwise generally good legibility. Shows bakehouses and exempt poor.

**Wentlooge hd.** [253/33](170). 1m. badly decayed and mostly illegible; other (120 names) OK.

***Subsidies***

**1661. Abergavenny hd.** [148/90](150). By street, VG.

**Usk hd.** [148/91](150). Flattened ms.

**1663. Caldicott hd.** [148/92](150). 3ms. sewn head to foot. Top ms. (Chepstow, Mathern) OK, but much decay (repaired) and illegibility in remainder of roll.

**Monmouthshire**: P.R.O., *Subsidies*, contd.

**1663. Wentlooge hd.** [148/93](70). Flattened ms., 2 sewn together. Top OK (Rumney, Michaelstone, St Mellons, Bassaleg, Newport), rest decayed.
**Ragland hd** [148/94](50). 2ms. sewn together. Top ms. OK (Clitha, Bryngwyn, Bettus Newith, Ragland, Tregare). Remainder decayed, repaired, but mainly illegible.

*Poll Tax*
**No date. County** [148/89](100). Fragments 2ms. legible and OK, 2ms. decayed and illegible.
**Wentlooge** [253/34](1,200). Roll, VG.

*Recusants*
**No date. Caldicott hd.** [253/35](52).

***Association Oath Rolls*, 1695** [C.213] [176] **County**; [177] Militia officers; [178] **Monmouth**; [179] **Newport**; [180] **Usk.**

## Norfolk

Publications

An exhaustive account of the surviving *Hearth Tax* records in the Public Record Office has been given by Peter Seaman (himself on the staff of the P.R.O.) in *The Norfolk Ancestor* in 5 parts, vol.2, pts. 2, 3, 5, 6, 9 (Sept 80 - June 82). This makes a detailed description of these records here unnecessary and inappropriate.

*Norfolk Hearth Tax Assessment, Michaelmas **1664***, transcribed by M.S. Frankel and P.J. Seaman, index by P.T.R. Palgrave-Moore, is published in *Norfolk Genealogy* vol.15, 1984? The introduction also describes the various HT records in the P.R.O. The **1664M** assessment was dispersed amongst six E.179 references [154/700, 707,709; 238/119; 253/45; 367/13]. Many of the ms. are in bad condition with poor legibility. Mr Seaman has remarked that 'the original records should only be examined by the serious scholar', and in the case of this meticulous transcript of what is clearly a very difficult source it should be necessary to see these documents only in exceptional circumstances. The assessment (which excludes Norwich) covers about two thirds of the county (23,500 names), the remainder being lost (Blofield, Brothercross hds., most of Gt. Yarmouth, and parts of other hundreds).

**Norfolk**, continued

*Norfolk and Norwich Hearth Tax **1666L*** [E.179/253/42-44], transcribed by P.J. Seaman, is published in *Norfolk Genealogy* **20** (1988). This covers most of Norwich and the hds. of Brothercross, Diss, Earsham, Gallow, Holt, Launditch, North Greenhoe, North Erpingham, Smithdon and Taverham; with partial returns for Clavering, Forehoe and Mitford hds.

'Norwich subscriptions to the voluntary gift of 1662' [E.179/154/655], transcribed by Miss P.M. Williams, Norfolk R.S.**1**(1931).

Public Record Office [E.179]

***Free and Voluntary Present*, 1661-2**

**County**, schedule of collectors' contributions [154/663](56); **Clavering hd.** [154/662](400); **Diss hd.** [153/618] (300); **North and South Erpingham, Eynsford and Holt hds.** [154/661](150); **South Erpingham hd.** [154/664](200); **Freebridge within Marshland** [154/653] (400), some fading; **South Greenhoe hd.** [154/651](140); **Happing hd.** [154/657] (150); **Henstead hd.** [154/659](150); **Holt hd.** [154/665](150)(see also above); **Launditch hd.** [154/660](300); **Loddon hd.** [154/658](150); **Lynn** [253/41](240); **Norwich** [154/655](500) (published); **Taverham, Blofield, South Walsham hds.** [154/654](300); **Tunstead hd.** [154/656] (200); **Wayland and Grimshoe** [157/12] (200); **'County'** [253/40](3,000). Six rolls, mostly short and easy to use, but one very long and unwieldy. Mostly good legibility, but occasional decay and poor legibility. Incl. **Great Yarmouth** (in paper book, VG).

*Hearth Tax*
The documents are described in detail by Peter Seaman in *The Norfolk Ancestor* and in the introduction to the edition of the Norfolk **1664M** assessment.

**1662M. Norwich** [154/701]. In poor condition.
**1664M. County**. Published, see left.
**1666L. County and Norwich** [253/42-44]. Published, see above.
**1672M. County** only (not Norwich) [154/697]. Badly damaged by rats, repaired but much lost.
**No date. Clavering** and **Depwade hds.**, Barton Bendish in **Clackhose hd.** [154/703a]. In reasonably good condition, one corner eaten away.
**Depwade, Diss, Earsham, Eynsford hds.** [154/704]. Same assessment and condition as previous reference.

**Norfolk**: P.R.O., *Hearth Tax*, contd.

*(Exemption certificates)*

**1671. Smithdon hd.** [154/696]. Paper. Sedgford (48) and Stanhow (28) only.

**1672-74. County and Norwich** [336]. Paper, many printed. Listed by hd. and parish, number of names and date, in *Norfolk Ancestor*, vol.2, pts. 6 & 9.

***Subsidies***

**1663. South Erpingham hd.** [154/666] (150). Some loss from decay, repaired.

**North Erpingham, North Greenhoe hds.** [154/667](300).

**Eynsford, Holt hds.** [154/668](?500). Bad condition, mostly illegible.

**No date. Smithdon hd.** [154/710](150).

**Eynsford hd.** [153/615](250).

***Poll Tax***

**1660.** Mainly schedules of arrears but may include some assessments. All refs. [E.179/**154**] followed by number shown: [633] Yarmouth (500), variable condition and legibility; [634] Yarmouth (350), end of ms. decayed; [635] S. Greenhoe and Grimshoe hds. (?350); [636] N. & S. Erpingham hds. (25); [637-8] Yarmouth (1,000); [639] Scratby (25); [640] Thrigby (40); [641] Winterton (37); [642] Clippersby (25); [643] Thurne (34); [644] East Somerton (15), damaged by damp, some names lost; [645] Billockby (18); [647] Yarmouth (400); [648] Herringby (25); [649] Stokesby (50), faded and some names lost from damp; [650] Deepwade hd. (425); [706] Diss hd. ( ? ), mostly illegible.

Ref. [E.179/**253**/38] Yarmouth (poor legibility), Askham cum Owby and Runham (200); [253/38a](320): Sturston, Santon Ho., Bucknam Ho., Sweeting cum Broomhill, Northwold, Methwold, Cranwith, Mundford, Colweston, Igborowe, Standford, Croxton, Merton, Breckles, Watton, Saham Tony, Carbrook, Thompston, Griston, Caston, Threpton, Ellingham cum Rockland, Stowbedon, Tetington, Ashill; [253/38b] Hemsby (90); [276/69b] Martham.

**1667.** Certificates of defaulters.

**Blofield hd.** [154/671](5);

**Ditchingham hd.** [154/690](23).

**(1678). County.** Certificates of defaulters, etc. [154/698](?250). Mainly collectors' names but short list of Yarmouth taxpayers.

**No date. County** [253/46](2,500). ?If Poll Tax. Much decay, repaired, legibility variable, but parts OK.

**Norfolk**: P.R.O., continued

***Association Oath Rolls*, 1695** [C.213]
[181] **County**; [182-84] **Norwich**; [185] **Kings Lynn**; [186] **Yarmouth**; [187] **Thetford.**

Norfolk Record Office, Central Library, Norwich NR2 1NJ.

**Norwich** city records include:

List of signatories against the Solemn League and Covenant, 1677-1718.

Books of assessments for the "Royal Ayde", 1664-1725.

Papers relating to hearth tax, 1666-96.

Hearth Tax (incomplete), 1671.

Supply, St John Maddermarket, 1678.

Royal aids, 1689 and 1691.

Poll Tax, St Peter Mancroft and St Stephen, 1694.

For the King's Navy, St Saviour, 1699-1700.

Subsidy. St Clement, 1702.

***Marriage Tax***

**Tunstead hd., 1704** [Pet 1047/20/1-26, 266x2] (except Hoveton St John);

**1705** [Pet 1047/21/1-23, 266x2] (except Barton Turf, Beeston St Lawrence and Sloley).

**King's Lynn** borough records (Regalia Room, Town Hall, King's Lynn; available by arrangement with Norfolk Record Office):

*Poll Tax* assessments, 1689, c.1690, 1714.

Tax assessments, 1702-05.

## Northamptonshire

Publication

*Hearth Tax* for **Grimsbury** and **Nethercote** (N'hants. part of Banbury (Oxon.) parish), **1662M, 1674L** [P.R.O. E.179/254/11,14], included in 'Taxpayers in Restoration Banbury', *Cake & Cockhorse* (Banbury Historical Soc.), vol.9, no.6.

Public Record Office [E.179]

***Free and Voluntary Present*, 1661-2**

**County** [254/9](3,000). Enrolled. Arrears [254/10](60).

***Hearth Tax*** *(Assessments and returns)*
(Microfilm copies at Northants. R.O.)

**1662M. County** [254/11](12,500). Enrolled. Occasional fading at edges of ms.
**Nassaburgh liberty** [254/12](1,750). Enrolled.
**(1662)M. Northampton** [254/15](500). Paper book. By ward.
**1663M** or **1664L. Nassaburgh hd.** [157/450] (1,000). Ms. sewn end to end, awkward to use.
**1670M. County** [157/446](22,000). Good condn. and leg., but 'imperfect'.
**1674L. County** [254/14](24,000). Enrolled. Some decay at edges.
*(Auditor's papers)*
**1662M-1663M** or **1664L. County** [157/468]. A miscellaneous collection of paper books (and one parchment m.), mostly accounts, but including lists of those in arrears at 1663M. Would repay detailed study.
*(Arrears)*
**1662M. County**. Sperate [372/2](50); desperate [372/3](100), faded; both in Latin.
**1663M. County**. Sperate [372/4](60); desperate [372/5](500). Both in Latin.

***Subsidies***
**(1663). Willibrook, Polebrook, Navisford hds.** [254/13](230).
**(1664). Corby, Rothwell, Huxloe, Orlingbury, Higham Ferrers** and **Hamfordshoe hds.** [157/448](1,000).
**No date. Corby** and **Rothwell hds.** [157/463](100). Parts badly faded.
**Nassaburgh hd.** [157/464](50). 1m. decayed and illegible, 1m. legible.

***Poll Tax*** *(?)*
**1660.** Castor [238/130](100). 1 flat m.
**No date. Nassaburgh hd.** [157/461](90). Fragment, 1 flat m., incl. Ailsworth, Sutton, Marholm.

***Association Oath Rolls*, 1695** [C.213]
[188] **County**; [189] **Peterborough**;
[190] **Northampton**; [191] **Brackley**;
[192] **Higham Ferrers.**

Northamptonshire Record Office, Delapre Abbey, Northampton NN4 9AW.

All *Hearth Tax* holdings at the P.R.O. are on microfilm at the N.R.O. [M.25/1,2].

***Parliamentary Aid***
**1691, Rothwell, Corby, Huxloe hds.** [M(TM)405-78].



***Poll Tax***
**1694-5. Rothwell hd.** [M(TM)479];
**Corby hd.** [C(TM)89].
**1698. Rothwell, Corby hds.** [C(TM)91-2];
**Huxloe hd.** [M(TM)480].

***Marriage Tax***
**1697. Rothwell hd.** [C(TM)90]. Transcript at N'hants R.O. and at the Society of Genealogists. Indexed.

***Window Tax***
**1702. Rothwell, Corby, Huxloe hds.** [C(TM)92].

The foregoing tax lists at the N.R.O., all in the Maunsell collection, have mostly been photocopied.

*Note*. Mr Francis Howcutt (22 Thurlestone Road, West Norwood, London SE27 0PD) is transcribing the surviving Northamptonshire Hearth Tax lists, concentrating on the parishes north of Northampton. He is at present unable to undertake searches, but would be glad to hear from anyone prepared to work on another defined part of the county.

## Northumberland

Publications

**Newcastle 1665** *Hearth Tax* [P.R.O. E.179/158/104](2,510 incl. exempt poor) in 'Newcastle Householders in 1665: Assessment of Hearth Tax', by Richard Welford, *Arch. Aliena*, s.3, vol.7, 1911, pp.49-76.

**Northumberland 1664** *Hearth Tax* [from photocopy 1925 at Northumberland R.O. of P.R.O. E.179/158/103], being published in *Jnl. of Northumberland and Durham FHS*, **8**, 3; **9**, 1, 2, 4; **10**, 1-11 *et seq.* (July 1983 on), transcribed by D.W. Smith. In progress.

Public Record Office [E.179]

***Free and Voluntary Present*, 1661-2**
**Berwick-upon-Tweed** only [272/37](174).

***Hearth Tax*** *(Assessments and returns)*

**(1662). County** [254/17]. Very badly decayed and much illegible.
**(1664). County** [158/103](3,500). Photocopy at Northumberland C.R.O. Being published in instalments, see above.
**1664L. Newcastle** [254/20](1,500). Flat parchment sheets. By ward.

**Northumberland**: P.R.O., *Hearth Tax*, ctd.

**(1664). Newcastle** [158/101](1,750). By ward. Shows exempt poor.
**1665L&M. County** [158/106](5,000). Includes exempt poor
**1665M. Newcastle** [158/104](2,510). Published, see p.35. Enrolled Jan 1666/7.
**1666L. County,** with **Newcastle** and **Berwick** [158/105](14,000). Repaired paper roll, VG.
**(1670-71). Newcastle** [158/109](150). Variations/alterations in assessment.
**1674L. Berwick-on-Tweed** [76/1](550). VG.
**(1674). County** [158/110](10,000).
**Newcastle** [254/21](?1,000).
First two ms. faded and illegible.
**No date. County** [254/22](8,000). 'Unfit for production'. Badly decayed in parts.
**County** [254/23]. Badly faded, decayed in part.
*(Exemption certificates)*
**1667-69.** Simonburn, Hartburn [360].
*(Arrears)*
**(1663). County/Newcastle** [254/19](750). By ward.
**(1664). County** [254/18](4,000).
**1662-64. Newcastle** [372/7,8](200). Constables' and sperate. Latin. Some fading and poor legibility.
**(1665). Newcastle** [158/102](750). Flat parchment ms.
**1666L. County** [158/99](1,500). VG.

***Subsidy***
**No date. County** [158/113](750). Sewn head to foot. VG.

***Association Oath Rolls*, 1695** [C.213] [193] **County**; [194] **Newcastle on Tyne**; [195] Militia officers; [196] Trinity House; [197] **Morpeth**; [198] **Berwick**; [199] **Alnwick**; [200] **North Shields**, etc.

Northumberland County Record Office, Melton Park, North Gosforth, Newcastle upon Tyne NE3 5QX.

Photocopy of *Hearth Tax* **1664** [N.R.O. 1925, of P.R.O. E.179/158/103]. Being published in instalments, see page 35.

*Note*. Transcripts of Hearth Tax reported to be in the possession of the Society of Antiquaries of Newcastle upon Tyne are in fact only incomplete extracts.

## Nottinghamshire

Publications

*Hearth Tax*, **County, 1664L** (dated 15 Jan 1663/4)[P.R.O. E.179/160/320-2, 254/28](10,473)(except Nottingham town); **1674L** [E.179/254/30,31](11,888). Exempt poor shown for both years. Indexed. Transcribed by W.F. Webster. Thoroton Society **37** (1988). The 1674L return for Nottingham (only) is also in *Chapters of Nottinghamshire History*, by J. Potter Briscoe (1908) (not indexed).

*Subsidy/Aid*, **1689** [Notts. R.O. DD MH 1/1-97]. First published as *Nottinghamshire Subsidies 1689*, ed. George Marshall, 1895. Re-edited by W.F. Webster and published by Notts FHS, records series vol.24, pts. 1 and 2, 1983 (now out of print). Indexed. Part of county only.

*Aid*, **1689-90** [P.R.O. E.179/254/34a] (1,000). **Broxtowe hd.** (39 places). Notts FHS vol.50, transcribed by W.F. Webster.

*Association Oath Rolls* ***1695*** [P.R.O. C.213/201-204]. For county (nobility, gentry, clerics) and Nottingham, East Retford and Newark (general inhabitants). Notts FHS vol.50, transcribed by W.F. Webster.

Public Record Office [E.179]

***Hearth Tax*** *(Assessments and returns)*
(Microfilms of documents for 1663, 1664 and 1674, as published, are at the Nottinghamshire Record Office.)

**1662M. County** except North Clay divn. of Bassetlaw [254/27](?5,500). Flattened parchment ms. bound in 6 parts, each with contents list by CAFM. Considerable decay, repaired, and some fading at feet of ms. Otherwise adequate legibility.
**(?1662). Bingham hd.** [160/329](400). Eleven palces only.
**Thurgarton hd.** [160/330](1,300). Most of hd. (54 places).
**Newark hd.** [254/33](1,250). Badly decayed, but many names legible.
**Bingham** and **Rushcliffe hds.** [254/34] (1,000). A duplicate of parts of 160/329 and 160/331. Small parts eaten away, but mainly legible.
**1664L. County** (except Nottingham). **Hds.** of **Bassetlaw** [160/322]; **Broxtowe, Rushcliffe** and **Bingham** [254/28]; **Thurgarton** and **Newark,** and **Newark** town [160/320]. Published, see above.

**Nottinghamshire:** P.R.O., *Hearth Tax*, ctd.

**(1670). Bassetlaw** and **Broxtowe hds.** [254/29](1,800). Incl. North Clay div. (5 places), Broxtowe hd. (17 places?) and Bassetlaw hd. (Hatfield div., 17 places?, South Clay div. 29 places?). Decayed in parts, repaired.

**1674L. County** [254/30](10,919). Published, see left.

**Nottingham** [254/31](969). Published, see left.

*(Arrears)*

**1663. Nottingham** and **County** [160/321] (250). Sperate arrears.

*Subsidies*

**(1664). Bassetlaw hd.** [160/323](500). Decayed and/or faded in parts.

**No date. Bassetlaw hd.** [160/324](100). 1ms. reasonable OK, remainder decayed and illegible.

*Aid*

**1689-90. Broxtowe hd** [254/34a](1,000). Published, see left.

*Association Oath Roll,* ***1695*** [C.213] [201-204]. Published, see left.

Nottinghamshire Record Office, County House, High Pavement, Nottingham NG1 1HR.

*Hearth Tax*

**?1661. Bassetlaw hd.** [DD.3P 18/1]. North Clay, South Clay and Hatfield divns. This is definitely dated '1661' and also described as 'Hearth Money', though the Tax was not introduced until 1662.

**1670. Arnold** [DD 241/11]. Typescript copy of P.R.O. E.179/254/29 (70).

*Subsidies*

**1663. Bassetlaw hd., Newark hd.** (part) [DD.N 230].

**1671, 1673. Eakring** [DD.SR 216/9-10].

*Subsidy/Aid/Land Tax*

**1689. County** (part only)[DD MH 1/1-97]. Published, see left.

*Land Tax*

**1697-1707.** West Bridgford [DD.PF 123107-108].

## Oxfordshire

Publications

*Hearth Tax* for **County, 1665M** [P.R.O. E.179/164/513](9,000) in *Hearth Tax Returns, Oxfordshire, 1665*, ed. Maureen M.B. Weinstock, Oxfordshire Record Soc. vol.21, 1940. The introduction discusses alternative records for 1662 and 1665. **Appx.A**: totals only, comparison of 1665M and 1662M [E.179/255/4] for Ploughley, Lewknor, Binfield, Bloxham, Wootton and Bampton hds.; **Appx.B**: transcript of *Subsidy* return for **Bullingdon hd., 1663** [E.179/164/503](400); **Appx.G**: *Poll Tax* return for **Taynton, 1666** (160)[original lost]; *Hearth Tax* **1662M** for **Taynton** [E.179/255/4](34). Index of places only.

Index of personal names to above book, *Index to Oxfordshire Hearth Tax Returns, Michaelmas 1665*, compiled by Jeremy Geere, Oxfordshire FHS, 1985 (£1.75 from J.S.W. Gibson, as back cover).

*Hearth Tax* for **Oxford** city, **1665L** [P.R.O. E.179/164/514](998) in *Surveys and Tokens*, ed. H.E. Salter, Oxford Historical Soc., vol.75, 1923, pp.183-212. Salter suggests this is for 1665**M** for no reason except that the 1662 return [255/4] was for Michaelmas. As 164/513 is specifically dated 1665**M**, it seems likely that 164/514 is for 1665**L**. This return was first published in Oxford Historical Soc., vol.18, 1890-1. pp.75-95, ed. T. Rogers (indexed), but the later edition contains corrections and is more logically arranged.

Vol.75 also includes an *Aid* for **1667** [Oxford City Archives, P.5.8](1,600), pp.337-54, and a *Poll Tax* for **1666/7** [City Archives, P.5.7](8,566), pp.213-336. Indexed. Not incl. St Clements.

**Banbury** (incl. Neithrop and Grimsbury): 'Taxpayers in Restoration Banbury', by J.S.W. Gibson, *Cake & Cockhorse* (Banbury Historical Soc.), vol.9, no.6 (Summer 1984), lists alphabetically all names (292) appearing in the *Free and Voluntary Present* **1661** [P.R.O. E.179/255/5], the *Hearth Tax* of **1662M**, Constables' returns [E.179/255/4; Grimsbury, Nhants, enrolled return, E.179/254/11], **1665L&M** [E.179/164/514,513] and **1674L** [Grimsbury, Nhants, only, E.179/254/14], and *Subsidy* for **1663** [E.179/164/507]. Hearths, sums paid, spellings, etc, compared.

**Caversham** - see Berks., with Reading.

*Association Oath Roll*. Banbury (*C&CH* **10**,4); Woodstock (*Oxon FH* **4**,2).

**Oxfordshire**, continued

Public Record Office [E.179]

***Free and Voluntary Present*, 1661-2**

**County** [255/5](many). Most (?all) of county in large and unwieldy roll. Several separate ms. (?duplicates, arrears) and one paper book (**Ewelme hd.**). The roll for **Oxford** appears to be *signed* by at least some of the contributors. **Banbury** published.

***Hearth Tax*** *(Assessments and returns)*

**1662M. County** [255/4](?10,000). Constables' paper returns, repaired and bound together, in three books. Arranged by hd.; VG and easy to use. Weinstock comments adversely, but for Banbury (published) these gave far more names and greater accuracy than the 1665 enrolled returns.

**County** [255/3](many). Constables' paper returns. Loose sheets, repaired. No special order. Not clear if these are duplicates of or additional to 255/4.

**Henley-on-Thames** [255/6]. Paper book, repaired, VG. Not clear if duplicate of or additional to 255/4.

**County** [164/504]. Enrolled copy. Badly decayed (eaten by rats), legibility difficult. Better to use 255/4.

**1665L. County** [164/514](8,000). Early ms. faded and in bad condition. Oxford city and Banbury published.

**1665M. County** [164/513](9,000). Includes exempt poor. Published, see page 37.

*(Arrears)*

**1663M. County** [372/10](75). Sperate.

**1664L. Bullingdon, Ewelme, Bloxham hds.** [164/506](75). Mainly constables' names.

***Subsidies***

**1663. Bullingdon, Thame, Dorchester hds.** [164/503](1,000). Parchment book. Bullingdon hd. published, see page 37.

**Banbury** and **Bloxham hds.** [164/507](300). Banbury parish published, see page 37.

**1664/5. Banbury** and **Bloxham hds.** [164/509](150). Flat parchment sheet. In four columns, first column (incl. Banbury town) decayed (repaired) and illegible, remainder OK.

***Association Oath Rolls*, 1695** [C.213]

[205-06] **County**; [207] **Postcomb**; [208] **Oxford**; [209] **Woodstock** (pubd., *Oxon FH*); [210] **Banbury** (pubd., *C&CH*).

Bodleian Library, Oxford

*Hearth Tax*. **1662M. County** [Microfilm, MS Film 182, of P.R.O. E.179/255/4].

Oxford City Archives, c/o Oxford Central Library (Local Studies), Westgate, Oxford OX1 1DJ.
(48 hours' notice required)

***Various taxes***, *etc.* (City and Binsey; not St Clement's parish)

**1667.** *Poll Tax* [P.5.7](8,566). Published, Oxford Historical Soc., **75**, see p.37.

**1667-68.** *Aid* [P.5.8](1,500). Six assessments between Sep 1667 and Dec 1668. One published in Oxford Hist. Soc. **75**.

**1692-94.** *Poll Tax* [P.5.9](1,500). Six assessments for the three years, and appeals.

**1694.** *Poll Tax* [P.5.10](1,500); **1695/6**, appeals only. **1696**, *Aid* (2,000). **1696**, *Window Tax* (1,500). Subsequent years give parish totals and collectors' names only.

**1695.** *Marriage Tax* [P.5.10, back end of book](210). Actual names, by parish. Total sums only for each parish, 1697, 1699, 1700, 1702, 1703, 1704, 1705.

**1702.** *Poll Tax* [F.4.6](3,250). Book gives names by parishes (as do all the above) followed by column for value of stock in trade, money at interest, pensions and annuities, offices @ 1s. in £, professions, practices and employments (sums of money only), 4s. per head, yearly rents and offices, sum to be charged.

## Rutland

No published sources, but transcript of *Hearth Tax* at Leicestershire R.O.

Public Record Office [E.179]

***Free and Voluntary Present*, 1661-2**

**County** [255/7](1,500). Ms. sewn head to foot.

***Hearth Tax*** *(Assessments and returns)*
(Microfilm copies of all references are at the Leicestershire Record Office)

**1664M. County** [255/9](3,200). Flattened parchment sheets, annotated.

**1665L. County** [255/11]. As 255/10.

**1665M. County** [255/10](?3,500). Exempt poor included.

*(Arrears)*
See Leicestershire, page 27.

***Subsidies***

**(1663). County** [165/195](300). Badly decayed but repaired and usable.

**East hd.** [255/8]. Too fragile to examine.

**Rutland**: P.R.O., continued

***Association Oath Roll*, 1695** [C.213] [211] **Rutland.**

Leicestershire Record Office, 57 New Walk, Leicester LE1 7JB.

*Hearth Tax*

All P.R.O. *Hearth Tax* holdings listed left are on microfilm at the Leicestershire Record Office [MF/130].

*Transcript:* **County, 1664M** [from P.R.O. E.179/255/9]. TS, by A.B. Clarke, 1948, names index by C.V. Appleton, 1949. Hds. of Alstoe, East, Oakham Soke, Martingley and Wrangdike.

## Shropshire

Publications

*Hearth Tax*, **1672M, County** [P.R.O. E.179/168/216](16,380, originally 17,737), in *The Shropshire Hearth-Tax Roll of 1672: being a list of the Householders in the County*, transcribed by Miss L. Drucker with an introduction by W. Watkins-Pitchford, Shropshire Arch. and Parish Register Soc., 1949. Paupers not identified. Fully indexed. List of 60 places missing from roll.

*Poll Tax* for **Ludlow, 1667** [P.R.O. E.179/255/37](1,300), in 'The Ludlow Poll Tax Return of 1667', Shropshire Arch. Soc. *Transactions*, No.59, 1972, pp.104-123. Includes two HT exemption certificates [presumably from E.179/342]. Not indexed.

'The Late 17th Century Tax Lists of the Borough of Shrewsbury and its Liberties', by Janice Capewell, *Shropshire FHS Journal*, **5**, 2 (June 1984).

Public Record Office [E.179]

***Free and Voluntary Present*, 1661-2**
**County** [168/214](7,500). Not obviously arranged by place, so probably difficult to use.

***Hearth Tax*** *(Assessments and returns)*

**1662M. County** [255/35](8,500). Decay at feet of ms., repaired. Much fading but most adequately legible. Introduction and contents list by CAFM.
**Brimstree hd.** [255/23](?750). Paper returns by constables, separate sheets, in roll. Slight decay in places.
**Albrighton** [358](50). Constable's paper return (stray).

**Shropshire**: P.R.O., *Hearth Tax*, contd.

**1663M. County** [255/24](many). Paper returns in bundles in no obvious order; incl. lists of exempt poor and schedule of arrears.
**1672M. County** [168/216](16,380, originally 17,737). 1m. lost, feet of many ms. mutilated. Published, see left.
**?1662-?1674. ?County** [342](many). A box full of a great many paper rolls, constables' returns, exemption certificates, etc., 1662-1670s. No attempt made at detailed examination.
*(Arrears)*
**1662-1664. County** [255/33,34; 373/1-7] (900 in all). Usually in Latin, few names apart from constables.

***Subsidies***
**(1663). Oswestry hd.** [255/25](21).
**(1664). North Bradford hd.** [255/26](200).
**Ford hd.** [255/27](80).
**Ludlow** [255/28](28).
**Oswestry hd.** [255/29](120).
**Pimhill hd.** [255/30](130).
**Shrewsbury** [255/31](250).
**Stottesden** and **Brimstree hds.** [255/32] (250).
**(1666). Bradford hd.** (northern part) [168/215](196). Dated 18 CII on cover, but ?1671 inside.

***Poll Tax***
**(1660). Wenlock** [168/219](2,500).
**South Bradford hd.** [168/220](5,000).
**North Bradford hd.** [255/21](5,000).
**Chirbury, Clun** and **Purslow hds.** [255/22](5,000).
**(1667). Ludlow** [255/37](500). Published, see left.
The foregoing poll tax lists indicate wives, give servants' names, etc.
**1678. County** [168/217](300). Poll Tax or Aid? Mainly collectors' names only, but some lists of ?defaulters, incl. some for Shrewsbury.

***Association Oath Rolls*, 1695** [C.213]
[212] **County**; [213] Militia officers; [214] **Shrewsbury**; [215] **Bridgnorth**; [216] **Ludlow**; [217] **Wenlock**; [218] **Bishops Castle**; [219] **Oswestry.**

Shropshire Record Office: Shrewsbury Borough archives - see page 40.

Shropshire Record Office, The Shirehall, Abbey Foregate, Shrewsbury SY2 6ND.

**Shrewsbury Borough Records** (see 'The Late 17th Century Tax Lists of the Borough of Shrewsbury and its Liberties', Janice Capewell, SFHS *Jnl* **5**.2). This is a particularly good collection of tax lists. All the bundles cover the town and the 'Liberties' (some 45 places, the equivalent of a hundred) unless otherwise stated. Most are Aids or Subsidies of some sort; other taxes indicated. All references should be preceded by '3365'.
*** = a large, full bundle of lists;
** = a middling size bundle of lists;
* = a small bundle of lists.

239-40. **1660.** Poll Tax ***.
241-42. **1661.** *.
243. **1662.** Some Liberties only *.
244. **1663.** *.
245. **1663.** Town only *.
246. **1664/5.** ***.
247-51. **1665-7.** **.
253. **1672-7.** ***.
254. **1673.** *.
255. **1678.** Poll Tax ***.
256. **1679.** *.
257. **c.1680.** One list for town only *.
258. **1689.** Poll Tax ***.
259. **1689.** Trophies money, Town only*.
260-61. **1690-2.** ***.
263. **1694.** Poll Tax ***.
264. **No date.** One list for part of Liberties only (incomplete)*.
266. **1697.** Castle Ward in town only *.
267. **1698.** Poll Tax ***.
268. **1702.** Poll Tax/Land Tax ***.
269. **1702.** Poll Tax, Stone Ward in town only *.
272. temp. Anne? Collector's book, Castle Ward in town only *.

***Marriage Tax***
275-79. **1695-1702.** *Full* censuses of the *whole* population ***. The S.R.O. has a transcript of the tax lists for the town.

***Land Tax***
280. early C18. *.

***House and Window Tax***
289. **1698-9.** ***.
290. **1710.** Abbey Foregate only *.
291. **c.1715.** Welsh and Castle Wards*.

**Bridgnorth**
**1689.** Poll Tax [SRO 4001/f/8/164]***.



Staffordshire Record Office, County Buildings, Eastgate St, Stafford ST16 2LZ.

**Munslow hd.**, co Salop., subsidy book, **1641-1664** [D(W)1788 p.46 6.8].
**Church Stretton**, co. Salop., *Poll Tax*, [D(W)1788 p.46 6.8].

## Somerset

(for **BRISTOL** see under Gloucestershire)

Publications

*Free and Voluntary Present* ***1661-2***, **Williton and Freemanors**, and **Carhampton hds.** [P.R.O. E.179/256/10](750), in 'A Benevolence granted to Charles II by the Hundreds of Williton and Freemanors and Carhampton', by Emanuel Green, Somerset A.S., **35**, 1889, pp.52-83. Not indexed.

*Hearth Tax*, **1665M**, for **County** [P.R.O. E.179/256/16](5,400). Published in *Hearth Tax for Somerset, 1664-5*, transcribed by R. Holworthy, *Dwelly's National Records*, vol.1, 1916. Annotated. Indexed. [Also includes E.179/172/440, 172/485, 256/18-20, 270/36.]

*Subsidy*, **1663**, for **Abdick, Crewkerne, Kingsbury East** and **South Petherton** [P.R.O. E.179/256/17](800) and certificates of exemption(?)[E.179/172/441] (200), published in *Dwelly's National Records*, vol.2, *Directory of Somerset*, trans. by E. Dwelly, 1929, pt.1, pp.1-32.

*Hearth Tax*, Exemption Certificates, **1670** [P.R.O. E.179/172/434 and Bundle 343] *Dwelly's National Records*, vol.2, pt.1 (1929), pp.32-64, **Abdick and Bulstone** to **Catsash hds.** (3,250); pt.2 (1929), pp.65-128, **Chew Magna** to **North Curry hds.** (6,400); pt.3 (1931), pp.129-192, **North Curry** to **Williton and Freemanors hds.** (6,400); pt.4 (1932), pp.193-211, **Williton and Freemanors** to **Winterstoke hds.** (1,850);

Exemption certificates, **1673-74** [all Bundle 343], pp.211-56, **Abdick and Bulstone** to **Frome hds.** (4,500); pt.5 (1932), pp.257-320, **Frome hd.** to **Wellow hd.** (Wynterton parish)(6,400). Uncompleted.

*Dwelly's Index to the Somerset Hearth Tax Exemption Certificates of 1670 and 1674 with a Completion of Part 5 of Dwelly's National Records vol.2* (115 pp.), published by T.L. Stoate, 1976. This completes vol.2 with an index to the whole volume, from the original at the Society of Genealogists.

Public Record Office [E.179]

*Free and Voluntary Present*, **1661-2**

**Houndsborough, Tintinhull, Martock, Somerton** and **Stone hds.** [172/424] (1,000). Paper book, VG.
**Wells Forum, Glaston** and **Whitston hds.** [256/9](1,000). Paper book.
**Williton and Freemanors,** and **Carhampton hds.** [256/10](750). Paper book. Published in Somerset A.S., vol.35.
**Bruton, Catsash, Norton Ferris** and **Horethorn hds.** [256/11](1,100). Paper book.
**Whitley, Huntspill, North Petherton, Andersfield** and **Cannington hds.** [256/12](1,250). Paper book.
**Bridgwater** [256/13](200). Paper book.
**Chew, Chewton** and **Keynsham hds.** [256/14] (400). Paper book. Transcript by Dwelly at Society of Genealogists.
**Frome, Kilmersdon, Wellow** and **Bath Forum** [256/15](350). Paper book.

*Hearth Tax (Assessments and returns)*

**1665M. County** [256/16]. Twelve hundreds only, in 18 books. Published, see left. Based on 1662M return.
**No date.** 'County'[256/20](150). In bad condition but legible: for Dinington, West Bradley, Charleton, Rill als Pill. Published in *Dwelly*, vol.1.
**Keynsham hd.** [172/440](200). Flat ms. Published in *Dwelly*, vol.1.

*(Exemption certificates)*

**1670. County** (except Bath Forum)[343] (very many). Printed paper forms. Published, see left.
**1674. County** [172/434](many). Printed paper forms. Published, see left.

*(Arrears)*

**1662M. County** [373/8,9]. Constables' and sperate. Latin.

*Subsidies*

**1663. Abdick, Crewkerne, Kingsbury East** and **South Petherton hds.** [256/17] (?500). Published, see left.
**(1663). Andersfield, Cannington, Huntspill and Puriton, North Petherton** and **Whitley hds.** [172/422](2,750).
**(1663-4). Houndsborough, Tintinhull, Stone, Somerton, Martock, Coker** and **Pitney hds.** [172/423](800); [172/426] (1,500). Slight decay, repaired.
**No date. Frome, Kilmersdon, Bath Forum** and **Wellow hds.** [172/439](400). Some decay and fading, but mostly OK.



*Poll Tax*

**1660. Portbury, Bempstone and Hartcliffe,** and **Bedminster hds.** [172/416](2,500). Some ms. badly faded, but much OK.
**Brent** [172/417](150). Some decay, considerable fading, but parts OK.
**North Curry, Milverton, Taunton** and **West Kingsbury hds.** [172/418](2,000). Mainly OK, but some ms. badly faded and occasional decay.
**Winterston hd.** [256/7](900). Stained and faded, poor legibility.
**Bath** [256/8](900). Paper book.

*Association Oath Rolls*, **1695** [C.213]
[220] **County**; [221] Militia officers; [222] Nonconformists; [225] **Bath**; [226] **Taunton**; [227] **Bridgwater**; [228] **Minehead**; [229] **Ilchester**; [230] **Milburn Port**; [231] **Crewkerne**; [232] **Bruton**; [233] **Langport**; [234] **Axbridge**; [235] **Wellington**; [236] **Chard**; [237] **Yeovil**; [238] **Ilminster**; [239] **Frome Selwood**.

Somerset Record Office,
Obridge Road, Taunton TA2 7PU.

*Subsidies*

**Williton and Freemanors hd., 1665** [DD/WY Box 34].

*Aids, etc.*

Ruishton parish, 1683 [DD/SP 450].
Andersfield hd., 1696 [DD/DP 24/5a].
Wells, 1703 [DD/SAS PR 163].

*Poll Tax*

**Williton and Freemanors hd., 1666** [DD/WY Box 34].

*Window Tax*

Ashill, 1700 [D/P/ashl 23/3].

*Land Tax*

Biddisham, 1711 [D/P/bid. 2/1/1].
Lympsham, 1689, 1715 [DD/DN 185].
Minehead, 1710 [DD/L 1/51/26].
Wells borough, from 1679 [DD/FS 72].

*Marriage Tax*

Langford Budville, 1704 [DD/SF 1869].

## Staffordshire

Publications

*Hearth Tax*, **1665M**, for **County** [P.R.O. E.179/256/31], in Staffordshire Record Society *Collections for a History of Staffordshire*, William Salt Arch. Soc.
**Pirehill hd.**, 1921, pp.41-173 (6,500).
**Seisdon** and **Offlow hds.** (excl. Lichfield), 1923, pp.47-258 (10,500).
**Totmanslow hd.**, 1925, pp.155-252 (4,250).
**Cuttlestone hd.**, 1927, pp.1-79 (3,700). Names for **Rugeley** and **Brereton** alphabetically arranged and annotated.
All transcribed by E. Grogan. Published version entitled '1666', because finally dated 1 June 1666, and delivered between 9 Jan 1665/6 and 2 Apr 1666, but collected for 1665M. Exempt poor shown. Indexes to places but not personal names.
*Hearth Tax*, **Lichfield, no date** [P.R.O. E.179/256/35] (380), annotated, and **1662M**, exempt poor and arrears [E.179/324] (200), S.R.S., *Collections*, W.S. Arch. Soc., 1936, pp.143-77, transcribed by P. Laithwaite. Index to places but not to personal names.
*Hearth Tax*, **1665**, **Bushbury**, in *Bushbury Parish and People*, A.H. Chatwin, 1983. Not indexed.

Public Record Office [E.179]

*Note*. The class number for these documents is E.179; thus for the first below, it should read in full: E.179/179/329. All references must be preceded by E.179.

***Free and Voluntary Present*, 1661-2**

**County**, incl. **Lichfield** [179/329] (7,750). Lichfield by street.

***Hearth Tax** (Assessments and returns)*

**1662M. Totmanslow hd.** [179/331] (3,500). Some decay and fading.
**Pirehill hd.** [179/332] (3,500). Introduction by CAFM. Stafford, Hopton, Hilderson and Hulton wanting. Considerable decay, repaired, and fading, but much OK.
**1664L. Lichfield** [375/2] (?250). Badly decayed, repaired, and faded; very little legible.
**1665M. County** (excl. Lichfield) [256/31] (25,000). Published, see above.
**1671M. County** [256/33] (?500). Variations of assessment. Badly decayed, not repaired.

**Staffordshire**: P.R.O., *Hearth Tax*, ctd.

**1672M. County** (excl. Lichfield) [256/32]
1. **Pirehill hd.** (4,000). Roll. Considerable decay, not repaired. Some fading and poor leg., but much OK.
2. **Cuttlestone hd.** (1,500). Flat, some decay, as 1.
3. **Seisdon hd.** (1,750). Roll. Some decay, legibility OK.
4. **Totmanslow hd.** (2,750). Flat. Decay repaired, variable legibility. Contents list by CAFM.
5. **Offlow hd.** Virtually all missing.

**1673M. County** [179/328] (15,000).
**No date. Lichfield** [256/35]. Paper book. Published, see left.
**Lichfield**, The Close [256/36] (33). Book.
*(Arrears and Exemption certificates)*
**1662** (Nov). **Lichfield** [179/324] (200). Paper list of exempt poor, by street. Also arrears. Published, see left.
**1662M** (dated 1664). **Stafford**, and **Pirehill** and **Offlow hds.** [179/334] (250). Certificates of poverty, paper. Some decay.
**(1663). County** [256/28] (150). Arrears.
**1663M-1664L. County** [373/10-12]. Arrears.

***Subsidies***
**(1662). Stafford and Pirehill hd.** [179/330a] (250). Some decay and fading.
**(1663). Offlow hd.** [179/323] (200).
**No date. Pirehill hd.** [179/171a] (42).

***Poll Tax***
**(1660). Cuttlestone hd.** [256/27] (350). Paper book.
**(1671). Offlow hd.** [256/26] (3,300). VG.

***Association Oath Rolls*, 1695** [C.213]
[257] **Pirehill**, etc. [258] **Seisdon**, etc.; [259] **County**, Deputy Lieuts., etc.; [260] **Stafford**; [261] **Newcastle under Lyme**; [262] **Tamworth**; [263] **Uttoxeter and Lichfield.**

Staffordshire Record Office, Stafford.

***Poll Tax***
**Cuttlestone hd., 1666** [D260/M/E/429/19].
**Ranton Abbey, 1678** [D615/E(X)/4].
***Marriage Tax***
Bilston, **1695** [D667/3/1].
***Window Tax***
**Cuttlestone hd., 1711** [D260/M/E/429/19].

British Library (Dept. of Manuscripts).
***Poll Tax***
**Lichfield, 1691** [P52/2214 Harley 7022].

Warwickshire Record Office, Warwick.
***Land Tax***: **1692-3. Rugeley, Brereton** and **Cannock Wood** [Landor papers CR931/194].

Shakespeare's Birthplace R.O., Stratford.
**1690. Hamstall Ridware** [DR.18/22/6].

## Suffolk

Publications

*Hearth Tax*, **1674L**, for **County** [P.R.O. E.179/257/14](28,400), in *Suffolk in 1674*, ed. S.H.A. Hervey, Suffolk Green Books, No.11, vol.13, 1905. Exempt poor sometimes shown. Indexed.

'The *Hearth Tax* Returns for the Hundred of **Blackbourne, 1662M**' [Suffolk R.O., HD.1538](1,070) trans S. Colman, *Proc. of the Suffolk Inst. of Archaeology for 1971*, vol.32, pt.2, pp.168-192. Some constables' returns, some copies. Some include exempt poor. Not indexed.

*Association Oath Roll*, **1696. Ipswich** (by parish), *East Anglian Miscellany*, vols. 3 & 4 (1909-10).

Public Record Office [E.179]

***Free and Voluntary Present*, 1661-2**
**County** [257/7](5,000).

***Hearth Tax*** *(Assessments and returns)*

**1662** (Dec). **Blything hd.** [257/9](500). Constables' returns, paper.
**(1662). Ipswich,** St Stephen [257/8](50). Constable's return, paper.
**1663L&M. Bosmere, Claydon** and **Plomesgate hds.** [257/10](133). Constables' paper returns, for Aldburgh (54, non-payers?), Rendham (1), Bramford (61, payers), Bosmere and Claydon (17).
**1663L. Ipswich** St Peter [257/10a](103). Constable's paper return.
**1663M. County** [257/15](?5,000). Paper returns of constables.
**(1664). County** [257/12](25,000). Some decay, repaired, some fading. Exempt poor shown. Brief introduction and contents list by CAFM.
**1663-4** [358]. Miscellaneous constables' paper returns, unsorted.
**1665L. Ipswich** [257/13](750). Paper book, annotated, exempt poor shown. VG.
**1666L. County** [183/616](?5,000). Paper books, constables' returns. VG.
**1670M.** [183/605](200). Fragments, incl. Buers, Chillton, Loos hd. (decayed). 2ms. adequate legibility and condn.
**1674L. County** [257/14]. Published, see above. Decay to 1m. repaired.
**No date. County** [183/610](2,750). All ms. decayed in parts, but legibility and condition otherwise adequate to good.



**No date. County** [257/17](6,400). Mostly good condn and legibility, but some decay, not repaired. Exempt poor shown.
**County** [257/18](?5,000). Condition too bad to examine in detail. Not repaired.
**County** [183/612](?1,000). Miscellaneous collection, needing sorting. Varied condition and legibility.
*(Exemption certificates)*
**1670M.** Ilketshall St Andrew [183/600](15).
*(Arrears)*
**1663M. County** (part)[183/614](150). Latin.
**Hoxne, Hartismere, Wangford, Blything** and **Cosford hds.** [183/565](50). Latin.

***Subsidies***
**1663. Babergh hd.** [183/508](250).
**Blything hd.** [183/563](350). Some decay, repaired.
**Bury St Edmunds** [183/564](85). Flat.
**(1663). Risbridge hd.** [183/602](160). Flat.
**Thredwestry hd.** [257/11](180). Some decay, not repaired.
**No date. Blackbourne hd.** [257/16(1)](50). Ockley, Wooton, ...eningfield, Nurton. Some decay, not repaired.

***Aid****(?)*
**No date. Hartismere hd.** [239/184](51). Decayed on one side, affecting place-names: ...could, ...ngesett Brockford, ...ke Ashe, ...roome, ...waite; answers of five non-payers.

***Association Oath Rolls*, 1695** [C.213]
[264] **County** (24 parts and hundreds);
[265] **Ipswich**; [266] **Orford**;
[267] **Aldborough**; [268] **Bury St Edmunds**.

Suffolk Record Office,
County Hall, Ipswich IP4 2JS.

***Hearth Tax***
**1662M, Blackbourne hd.** [HD.1538](pub'd.).
***Window Tax***
**1715**, for parishes of Stuston, Redgrave, Burgate, Wyverstone, Thornham Magna, Rishangles, Thwaite, Thorndon and Occold [HD 79/AD1/3/9-18].

## Surrey

Publications

*Free and Voluntary Present* ***1661-2***, for **County** (excl. Brixton hd. and Southwark) [P.R.O. E.179/257/28](3,881), in *Calendar of the Surrey Portion of the Free and Voluntary Present to Charles II*, compiled by Cliff Webb, West Surrey Family History Society Record Series, vol.2, 1982. Indexed.

*Hearth Tax*, **1664L, County** (excl. Southwark) [P.R.O. E.179/188/481] (17,000), in *The Surrey Hearth Tax, 1664*, ed. C.A.F. Meekings, Surrey Record Soc., vol.17, 1940. Arranged alphabetically. The introduction includes sample transcripts of constables' returns and/or exemption certificates for **1662** [P.R.O. E.179/187/479] for **Ripley in Send, Kennington** in Lambeth, **Ockham, Woldingham** and **Wisley**; and for **1664M** [E.179/258/1] for the east half hd. of **Woking**, for **Send, East** and **West Horsley, Ockham, East** and **West Clandon, Ripley** in Send, and **Godalming**. The introduction has much of relevance nationally.

*Association Oath Rolls for Surrey, 1695*, transcribed by Cliff Webb, West Surrey FHS, Microfiche Series **3** (one fiche + booklet), 1990, £1.20.

See also *Surrey Inhabitants Lists*, West Surrey FHS Research Aid No.7.

Public Record Office [E.179]

***Free and Voluntary Present*, 1661-2**
**County** [257/28] (?5,500). Published, except for Brixton hd. and Southwark.

***Hearth Tax*** *(Assessments and returns)*

**(1662). County** [187/479] (many). Paper returns by constables and exemption certificates. Repaired, stitched into (?geographical) sections. VG.

**1662M-1663L. Lambeth, Prince's** and **Kennington liberties; Battersea, Merton, Putney, Tooting, Wandsworth, Wimbledon** [257/29] (?4,000). Constables' paper returns, bound into book form, easy to use, VG.

**1663. Brixton, Elmbridge, Godalming, Godley, Tandridge, Wotton** and **Woking hds.**, with **Guildford** and **Carshalton** [257/30] (?10,000). Constables' paper returns; loose sheets in six folders, by hd., etc.

**Farley** [256/29] (8). Constable's return.

**(1663). Bermondey** (pt.), **Bisley, Crowhurst, Worplesdon** [258/5] (200). Paper returns from constables. Also incl. Burham, Weeke, West End tithings.

**1664L. County** [188/481] (?25,000). Published, see above.

**Blackheath, Brixton, Copthorne, Farnham, Godley, Godalming, Reigate, Tandridge, Wallington, Wotton** and **Woking hds.** [258/1] (?20,000). Constables' paper returns and exemption certificates, bound as book. VG.



**1664. Leatherhead** area [SP.28/1/177; *not* in Class E.179].

**(1664-5). Southwark** [258/7] (2,500). Paper book.

**Reigate** [258/8] (500). Fragments, 2ms. only. 1m. decayed, not repaired, the other OK.

**1665L. Brixton hd.** [188/489a] (7,500). Annotated list. Considerable decay, repaired.

**1666L. Brixton hd.** [188/489b] (500). Considerable decay, poor legibility, but some OK and legible.

**(1669-70). Southwark: St Olave** (part), Upper Ground liberty, **St Saviour:** Clinke liberty; **Newington; Bermondsey; Lambeth** (1st page missing); **West Brixton half hd.; Wandsworth** (these contained the major part of **Southwark and Brixton hd.**); and hds. of **Blackheath, Copthorne and Effingham, Emleybridge, Farnham, Godley, Kingston, Reigate, Tandridge, Wallington** and **Woking** [258/4] (?25,000). Returns by constables, in 18 paper books. Occasional decay repaired. VG.

**Southwark St George's** [188/506] (650). Paper book, annotated, listed by street. VG.

**(1672-3). County** [188/504] (15,000). Some decay.

**1672-3. County** [188/494] (750). Paper exemption certificates.

**(1673). County** [188/496] (15,000). Exchequer duplicate. Double columns.

**Woking hd.** [258/6] (800). Constable's return, paper book, annotated.

*(Arrears)*

**(1662M-1663M). County** and **Southwark** [374/1-3] (1,000). Desperate.

**1664. Southwark** [188/485] (50).

**1670. County** [188/508] (?1,000). Draft paper schedule.

***Subsidies***

**(1663). Guildford** with **Farnham, Godalming, Godley, Blackheath, Woking** and **Wotton hds.** [188/480] (600). Considerable decay, repaired, but much lost.

**(1664). Elmbridge hd.** [187/476] (80). Some decay, repaired, fading. Poor leg.

**Kingston hd.** [188/484] (100). In bad condition, partly repaired.

**(1667). Southwark** [272/38] (70). Flat.

***Poll Tax***

**(1677). County** [188/502] (?250-500). Exemptions and arrears only.

**1689. Southwark, St George** [258/3] (26). Certificate of defaulters.

**Surrey**: P.R.O., continued

*Aid(?)*

**No date. County** [188/505](?1,000). Fragments, badly decayed, repaired, and faded.

***Association Oath Rolls*, 1695** [C.213] [269] **County**; [270a-270b] Deputy Lieuts. and **Southwark**; [271] **Bletchingley**; [272] **Reigate**; [273] **Gatton**; [274] **Kingston on Thames.**
Whole county published, see left.

Surrey Record Office, County Hall, Kingston upon Thames, KT1 2DN.

***Poll Tax***

**Leatherhead and Pachenesham liberty**, late 17th century [212/66/7].

Kingston Borough Archives, c/o Surrey Record Office.

***Poll Tax***

Walton on Thames (incl. Hersham), **1666** [KS1/1/1].

Guildford Muniment Room, Surrey Record Office, Castle Arch, Guildford GU1 3SX.

***Subsidy*, 1671**

Assessment for Artington, Binscombe, Catteshall, Chiddingfold, Compton, Eashing, Farncombe, Godalming town, Guildford (St N.), Hambledon, Haslemere, Hurtmore, Laborne, Peper Harow, Shackleford, Thursley, Tuesley and Witley (all West Surrey)[Loseley MSS. 1506/1-18]. Some in bad condition.

For **Southwark**, see also under **LONDON**.

## Sussex

Publications

*Hearth Tax*, **1670L** [P.R.O. E.179/191/410](531), **Chichester** city only, in *Sussex Archaeological Collections*, vol.24, 1872, pp.78-84, transcribed by W.D. Cooper. Not indexed.

*Hearth Tax*, **1662M, Lewes Rape** [based on 1664M, P.R.O. E.179/258/15](2,000); **Pevensey Rape** [based on 1665M, E.179/258/16](2,500), in *Sussex Hearth Tax Assessments 1662*. 1. ***Lewes Rape***; 2. ***Pevensey Rape***, both ed. M.J. Burchall, introduction in **1** by J.H. Farrant, Sussex Genealogical Centre, Occasional Papers Nos. 3 and 4, 1980. Not indexed.

*Aid*, **Rye, 1660** [E.S.R.O. RYE 82/82](670), in *The Sussex Genealogist*, vol.4, no.3, pp.97-108.

**Sussex**, continued

Public Record Office [E.179]

***Hearth Tax*** *(Assessments and returns)*
(Microfilms of P.R.O. holdings are at East Sussex Record Office)

**1664M. Bramber rape** [258/14](2,000). Paper book.
**Lewes rape** [258/15](2,000). Paper book. Published, see left.
**(?1664).** [191/416](1,500). Fragments, badly decayed but well repaired and now easy to use. Various locations, some identified.
**1664-5. Hastings rape** [258/20](700). Paper book, repaired. Annotated.
**1665M. Pevensey rape** [258/16](2,500). Paper book. Published, see left.
**Pevensey rape** [258/19](450). Paper book, annotated. ? if partial duplicate of 258/16.
**Bramber rape** [258/17](3,350). Nine paper books, annotated.
**Lewes rape** [258/18](3,600). Twelve paper books, annotated.
**1670L. County** [191/410](?10-15,000). In six parts, sewn at head. Much fading and decay, repaired. Notes by CAFM.
**No date. Hastings rape** [258/21](1,250). Paper book, annotated.

***Subsidies***

**(1664). Lewes rape** [191/409](300). Bad decay, repaired.
**No date. Chichester rape** [191/412] (?1,000). Decayed, repaired, at head of roll. Roll stitched head to foot. Variable legibility.

***Poll Tax***

**1660. Rye** [258/13](500). Parchment book. By ward, occupation given. VG. Probably a duplicate of Rye Corpn. Papers 82/82, see page 46.

***Association Oath Rolls*, 1695** [C.213]
(Mf of C.213/275-283 at W. Sussex R.O.)

[275] **West Sussex**; [276] **East Sussex**; [277] Grand Inquest; [278] **Chichester**; [279] **Midhurst**; [280] **New Shoreham**; [281] **Bramber**; [282] **Arundel**; [283] **Rye**; [332] **Cinque Ports.**

East Sussex Record Office, The Maltings, Castle Precincts, Lewes, E Sussex BN7 1YT.

***Hearth Tax***

All P.R.O. *Hearth Tax* holdings listed, except for E.179/258/14, are on microfilm at the East Sussex R.O.

**Sussex**: East Sussex R.O., continued

**Rye** Corporation archives (at E.S.R.O.) include ***Hearth Tax*** papers:
**1662M.** Assessment [83/1].
**1663.** Account of hearths [83/2-4].
**1664.** Assessment [83/5].
**1665.** Exemption certificates [83/6-11].

***Aid(?)*. 1660. Rye** [Corpn papers 82/82]. Published, see page 46.

West Sussex Record Office, County Hall, Chichester, West Sussex PO19 1RN.

Mf of *Association Oath Rolls* for Sussex [MF 710][P.R.O. C.213/275-283].

Kent Archives Office, Maidstone.

***Poll Tax*** **1666. Frant** [Powell MSS, U934].

## Warwickshire

Publications

*Hearth Tax*, **1662M-1674, Hemlingford hd., Tamworth** and **Atherstone divisions** [all relevant P.R.O. and Warwickshire R.O. references for this period](?3,000), in *Warwick County Records, Hearth Tax Returns*, vol.1, ed. Margaret Walker, 1957/8. Names from all available returns collated. Fully indexed. An immensely detailed introduction by Philip Styles reveals the complexity of the collections under different authorities and of giving these precise dates. Unfortunately no further volumes in this series appeared, and any further transcription done at that stage is not available to the public. However, the Warwickshire Record Office does have an index to the 1674 return, see below.

*Hearth Tax*, **1663** [Warwickshire R.O., Q.S.11/5], for Farnborough, Warmington, Mollington, Wormleighton, Shotteswell, Avon and Burton Dassett, Fenny Compton, Priors Hardwick and Ratley (420) in *Cake & Cockhorse* (Banbury Historical Society), vol.1, 1960, pp.45-48, 62-64, 78-79. Indexed.

*Hearth Tax*, **1662, 1671, Tysoe** [Warwickshire R.O., Q.S. 11/2, 11/?] in *The Parish Registers of Tysoe*, ed. D.B. Woodfield, 1976. Indexed.

*Poll Tax*, **1660, Knowle** [location of original now unknown](77) in *Records of Knowle*, 1914, pp.379-80.

Index (in Warwickshire Record Office)

***Hearth Tax*** **1674** (10,000). Whole **county.**

**Warwickshire**, continued

Public Record Office [E.179]

***Free and Voluntary Present*, 1661-2**
**County** [259/7](?15,000). Microfilm at Warwickshire R.O.
**Coventry** [194/326](349). Part arranged by ward. MS transcript at Coventry City Record Office.

***Hearth Tax*** *(Assessments and returns)*
(Microfilm or photostat copies of returns for 1664-5, 1666L, 1671M, 1673M and 1679-80 are at Warwickshire Record Office.)

**1664M-1665M?. County** [259/10](16,500). Annotated. Mostly in good condition, but a few ms. faded. Part published. [Styles' introduction, pp.42-44].
**1666L. County** [259/9](20,000). Paper book, annotated, forges, ovens, etc. shown. VG. Part published, see left. [Styles' introduction, p.58].
**1671M. Hemlingford hd.** [194/325](3,500). Considerable decay, repaired, and variable legibility [Styles' introduction, p.70]. Includes the greater part of the Birmingham division, missing from the county copy . Partly published, see left.
**Knightlow hd.** [194/338](?1,500). Much decayed, repaired.
**1673M. Hemlingford** and **Kington hds.** [259/12](1,250). Badly decayed, repaired. Notes by CAFM.
**(1679-80). Coventry, Fillongley** and **Coleshill** [259/11](800). Paper, repaired. Annotated. See *The Hearth Tax Collectors' Book for Worcester 1678-1680*, ed. C.A.F. Meekings, S. Porter and I. Roy, Worcs. Hist. Soc. N.S. vol.11, 1983, Introduction, page 12.
**1683/4. Birmingham** [375/1](243). Newly-erected and smiths' hearths, in Birmingham (by street), Erdington, Edgbaston, Bordesley, Castle Bromwich, Derrit End and Little Bromwich. VG. [Styles' introduction, p.97].

*(Arrears and exemption certificates)*
**1662M. County** [259/6](?500). Desperate arrears, in Latin.
**Coventry** [194/329](?1,500). Incl. long lists for Coventry. Parchment and paper.
**1663M. County** [374/4,5](125). Sperate and desperate. [Styles, intro., p.28].
**1662-66. County** and **Coventry** [194/327] (?150). Varied legibility, some annotations [many references in Styles' introduction].

**Warwickshire**: P.R.O., *Hearth Tax*, contd.

*(Exemption certificates)*
**(1671-2). County** [194/334](?2,000).Fragile.
**1671-74. County** [347][Styles, page 70].

*Subsidies*
**1663. Coventry** [259/8](250). By street.
**1663/4. Coventry** [194/330](171). By ward. Transcript at Coventry C.R.O.
**(1663). Hemlingford hd.** [194/328](?500). Considerable decay, repaired, but some parts legible (incl. Solihull).

***Association Oath Rolls*, 1695** [C.213] [284-85] **County**; [286] **Coventry**; [287] **Warwick**; [288] **Stratford**.

Warwickshire Record Office, Priory Park, Cape Road, Warwick CV34 4JS.

***Free and Voluntary Present*, 1661-2**
Microfilm of P.R.O. E.179/259/7.

*Hearth Tax*

TS index of **1674** return.
*Photostats* of P.R.O. returns for **1664-5** and **1666L** [E.179/259/10,9]; *microfilm* of P.R.O. returns for **1671, 1673, 1679-80** [E.179/325,338; 259/12,11].

*Original returns:*
**1662M. County** [Q.S.11/1-4](8,500). Part published. Part of Atherstone and all Birmingham missing. [Styles, pp.16-17]
**1663M. County** [Q.S.11/5](15,376). Part published. [Styles, pp.30-31.]
[The following returns, **1670-74**, are referenced Q.S. 11/7-59, consisting of 53 separate books. Part published. Styles' introduction, pages 69-75.]
**1670** (3 ½yrs 1669L-1670M). **County**.
**1671** (1670M-1671M). **Kineton hd; Hemlingford hd.**, Solihull, Tamworth and Atherstone divisions.
**1673** (3 ½yrs 1671M-1673L). **County**.
**1674** (1673L-1674L). **County** (10,000). Indexed.
**1682-4.** New hearths and forges, in **Birmingham, Deritend, Edgbaston,** liberties of **Aston** [Q.S.11/60-63]. [Styles' introduction, page 97].

*Poll Tax*
Wellesbourne Hastings, **1678** [CR 133/81].
Chilvers Coton, **1690** [CR 136/?].

*Aid*
**1692/3. Hemlingford hd., Atherstone** and **Tamworth divns.** [CR 136/C1646](1,700).

*Marriage Tax*
**Fenny Compton, 1698.** See 'A Census of a Warwickshire village in 1698', Philip Styles, *Birmingham Hist. Jnl.* **3**, 33-51.

**Warwickshire**: Warwickshire R.O., contd.

*Land Tax*
Hampton in Arden: Balsall, **1711** [CR 112/Ba 1456,148].
Wellesbourne Hastings, **1711** [CR 133/82] (25).

Coventry City Record Office, Room 220, Broadgate House, Broadgate, Coventry CV1 1NG.

Transcripts of the *Free and Voluntary Present*, ***1661-2*** [P.R.O. E.179/194/326] (349) and the *Subsidy*, ***1663/4*** [P.R.O. E.179/194/330](171), both of **Coventry** only.

Shakespeare Birthplace Trust Records Office, The Shakespeare Centre, Stratford upon Avon CV37 6QW.

*Hearth Tax*
Photocopies of returns for 1662, 1663, 1670, 1673, 1674 [PR 72][presumably from Warwickshire R.O. Q.S.11].

***Aids, Subsidies**, etc.* (originals)
Alveston, **1668** [DR 74/21].
Fillongley, **1690, 1692** [ER 65/21,22].
Stivichall, *subsidy*, **1671-2** [DR 10/1842].

## Westmorland

Publications

*Hearth Tax*, **1670M, County** [P.R.O. E.179/195/73](5,000) and **1663, Kendal** only [E.179/195/74](100), in *Records Relating to the Barony of Kendale*, vols. 1 and 2, by William Farrer and/or John F. Curwen (1923 and 1924), and *The Later Records relating to North Westmorland*, by J.F. Curwen (1932), also published by the Cumberland & Westmorland Antiquarian and Archaeological Society, records series vols. 4, 5 and 8. These volumes consist of miscellaneous abstracts of a variety of records, arranged by parish, but each parish entry includes the 1670M Hearth Tax, with Kendal additionally having that for 1663. Indexed.

Public Record Office [E.179]

*Hearth Tax*

**(1663). Kendal ward** [195/74](100). Badly decayed, not repaired. Published.
**1662M-1664L. County** [259/13](?500). Returns of defaulters. Incl. original constables' paper returns, and enrolled parchment copies in Latin.

**Westmorland**: P.R.O., *Hearth Tax*, contd.

**1670M. County** [195/73](5,000). Published, see page 47. Flat, short ms., some fading.
**No date. County** [259/14](3,500). Flat, short ms., some decay, much fading.

***Association Oath Rolls*, 1695** [C.213] [289] **Appleby**; [290] **Kirkby in Kendal**. See also Cumberland rolls.

Cumbria Record Office, County Offices, Kendal, Cumbria LA9 4RQ.

***Hearth Tax*** *(original)*
**1674. County**, excl. Kendal [WD/Ry Box 28]. A notebook of Sir Daniel Fleming.

***Marriage Tax***
**1695.** Lists of inhabitants for parishes in the **Lonsdale Ward**, and Highgate, Stramongate and Stricklandgate in the town of **Kendal** [WD/Ry Box 32].

## Wiltshire

Publications:

'Salisbury: A Royal Aid and Supply for 1667' (*Wilts A&NHS Mag.* **36** pp.413-34), indexed), reptd. in *Endless Street: A History of Salisbury*, J. Chandler, 1983.

Public Record Office [E.179]

***Hearth Tax*** *(Assessments and returns)*

**1662M. County** [259/29](11,000). In four parts, ms. sewn at top, flat. Much decay, repaired, and fading. The only full return for the county.
*(Exemption certificates)*
**1662M. County** [259/26b](1,000). Paper certificates from constables, bound into book. In good condition.
**County** [374/6](120). Enrolment on parchment of 259/26b. Latin.
**1673/4.** [360]. Miscellaneous.
*(Arrears)*
**1662M. County** [374/7](120). Latin.
**1671M. Malmesbury, Chippenham** and **Calne hds.** [199/424](50). Decayed but repaired and now in good condition and legible.

***Subsidies***
**1663. Dunworth, Mere** and **South Damerham hds.** [199/420](?500). Mostly badly decayed, repaired, and bad legibility. Only 1m. reasonably OK.
**1663/4. Warminster, Heytesbury, Whorwelsdown hds.** and **liberty of Deverill Longbridge** (pt. of Damerham South hd.) [199/421](500). Slight decay and some fading on some ms., generally OK.

**Wiltshire**: P.R.O., *Subsidies*, continued

**1664. Underditch, Downton, Cawden and Cadworth, Frostfield, Branch and Dole** and **Chalk hds.** [259/27](450). Good.

***Poll Tax***
**1660. Whorwelsdown hd.** [259/26a](96). Some decay at foot (? if Poll Tax).
**(1660). Salisbury** [199/419](2,000). Arranged by street. Some fading on final m., otherwise VG.
**Salisbury Close** [199/416](180). Flat.
**Bradford hd.** [199/418](200). Flat ms. Half very faded, part OK. (? if Poll Tax).
**No date.** [259/28](100). Boyton and Corton, Horningsham (decayed and faded), Boreham, Bishstrowe, Norton Bavent.

***Association Oath Rolls*, 1695** [C.213] [291] **County**; [292] Militia officers; [293] **New Sarum** (Salisbury); [294] **Wilton**; [295] **Downton**; [296] **Hindon**; [297] **Westbury**; [298] **Calne**; [299] **Devizes**; [300] **Chippenham**; [301] **Malmesbury**; [302] **Great Bedwin**; [303] **Ludgershall**; [304] **Marlborough**; [305] **Ramsbury**; [306] **Bradford.**

Wiltshire Record Office, County Hall, Trowbridge BA14 8JG.

***Marriage Tax*** [7202A WG8/]
(There are transcripts for asterisked returns at the Wiltshire R.O.)

[1] Broad Hinton, Binknoll tithing only, 1697, 1700, 1701; [2] Chisledon, 1697; [3] Chisledon with Draycot Foliat, 1700*, 1702, 1705; [4] Clyffe Pepard 1697, 1701*; [5] Hilmarton (except Catcomb tithing) 1697*, 1700, 1701*; [6] Liddington, 1697, 1700, 1702; [7] Lydiard Tregoze 1697, 1700, 1701; [8] Lyneham 1697*, 1700, 1701, 1702; [9] Swindon 1697*, 1701, 1702, 1705; [10] Tockenham 1697, 1700, 1701; [11] Wanborough 1697, 1700, 1702, 1705*; [12] Wootton Bassett 1697*, 1701*, 1702, 1705; [13] Little Hinton 1700; [14] Wroughton (incl. the five tithings in Kingsbridge) 1700, 1701*; [15] Wroughton (incl. town tithing only) 1697; [16] Wroughton (Elcombe and Uffcott tithings only) 1705.

Salisbury city records:
*Aid:* **1667. Salisbury.** [G.23/1/172]. Published, see left.

## Worcestershire

Publication

*The Hearth Tax Collectors' Book for* ***Worcester, 1678-1680***, ed. C.A.F. Meekings, S. Porter and I. Roy, Worcestershire Hist. Soc., N.S. vol.11, 1983 [P.R.O. E.179/260/13(1)](2,301). Indexed. Informative introduction which discusses the administrative records for both city and county.

Public Record Office [E.179]

***Hearth Tax*** *(Assessments and returns)*
(Microfilms of all Hearth Tax records are at the County Record Office)

**1662M. County** (excl. Worcester)[201/325] (?9,000). Flat ms. sewn at top, considerable decay at feet of ms., repaired, and staining and fading, poor legibility.
**County** (prob. excl. Worcester). [260/4] (many). Constables' paper returns, well repaired and bound in book form.
**1664L. County** (excl. Worcester)[260/16] (?5,000). Repaired but badly decayed and faded. Introduction by CAFM.
**Worcester** [201/323]. Decayed and mainly illegible.
**1664M-1665M** (revision of **1662M**). **County** (excl. Worcester)[201/312](10,000). Enrolled. Some decay, part repaired, fading and staining, but much OK. Exempt poor shown. Intro. by CAFM.
**Worcester** [260/8](890). Annotated. By ward.
**1666L. County** (excl. Worcester)[260/5] (4,500); [260/6](3,000).
**1671L. County** (excl. Worcester)[260/9] (7,500). Much decay (repaired) and fading. Poor condition.
**(?1671-2). County** (excl. Worcester) [375/15](5,000). Considerable decay, repaired, variable legibility but mostly OK. Brief introduction.
**1673L. Worcester** [260/12](1,000). Ms. sewn head to foot. Annotated. Some fading and damage.
**1674L. County** [260/10](11,500).
**Worcester** [260/11](1,024). Ms. sewn head to foot. Annotated. As 260/12.
**1679M-1680M** (based on **1678** assessment) **Worcester** [260/13(1)](2,301). Published, see above. [260/13(2)] consists of some loose paper leaves (150 names). Not clear if these are included in the published volume.
**Kidderminster** [260/14](500). paper book, VG. See *Worcester Hearth Tax*, Introduction, page 12.

**Worcestershire**: P.R.O., *Hearth Tax*, ctd.

*(Arrears and exemption certificates)*
**1662M. County** [374/8-10](275). Latin, constables', sperate and desperate.
**1663L. Worcester** [374/12](?75). Latin. Sperate.
**1663M. County** [201/317/2,3; 374/11](400). Latin. Constables', sperate, desperate.
**Worcester** [260/7](?250). Desperate.
**1663L&M. County** [201/317/1](very many). Paper exemption certificates, repaired and bound in two vols.
**1663-4. County** [201/318a]. Latin, 1664 (750). English, exemption certificates, annotated, 1663-4 (550).

***Subsidies***
**1660. County** [260/3*](1,000). Decay at feet of some ms. Part of Poll Tax ?
**1663. Halfshire hd.** [201/322](250).
**Pershore hd.** [201/319](400).
**(1663). Doddingtree hd.** [201/315a](300). Some decay, repaired. Considerable fading/staining, legibility variable.
**1664. Doddingtree hd.** [201/320](300).
**Worcester** [201/321](130).
**(1664). Evesham** [201/307](44). Some decay, repaired, but most names survive.

***Poll Tax***
**1660. Worcester** [270/21](3,000). Paper, well repaired and bound together, easy to use (photocopy at County R.O.).
**County** [274/10](?500-1,000). Paper. Incl. North and Middle Littleton, Gt and Little Hampton, Badsey, Offenham, Aldington, Bratforton, Evesham St Lawrence, Weckhamford, Littellton, Dengworth, Evesham All Saints, Lenchwick and Norton.

***Association Oath Rolls*, 1695** [C.213] [307] **County**; [308] **Worcester**; [309] **Droitwich**; [310] **Evesham**; [311] **Bewdley**; [312] **Kidderminster**.

Hereford and Worcester Record Office. At County Hall, Spetchley Road, Worcester WR5 2NP.

***Hearth Tax***
**1662M. Doddingtree hd.** [In Midsummer 1662 Quarter Sessions, packet no. 102, Documents nos. 1-33]. Constables' returns for 33 places.

At Worcester Branch, St Helen's, Fish Street, Worcester WR5 2HN.

Microfilm of all Worcs. and Worcester *Hearth Tax* records at the P.R.O.
Photocopy of the *Poll Tax*, **1660**, for **Worcester** [P.R.O. E.179/270/21].

## Yorkshire

Public Record Office [C.213]

***Association Oath Rolls*, 1695**
[313] **Yorkshire**; [314] **Yorkshire** (35 items). These two references probably relate to all three Ridings.

## York

Publication

'York in the 17th Century' by G.C.F. Forster, in *V.C.H.: City of York*, 162-5.

Public Record Office [E.179]

***Hearth Tax*** *(Assessments and returns)*

**1665. City and Ainsty** [260/20](?2,500).
**1671M. City** [260/21](2,000). Ms. sewn at head.
**1672. City** [260/22](2,124). Imperfect. Contents list by CAFM.
**No date. City** [260/23](84). Fragment. Acombe, Acaster Malbis, Acaster Selby.
*(Arrears)*(see also page 53)
**(1663). City** [270/52](700). Latin.
**1664. City and Ainsty** [218/211](550). Latin.

***Subsidy***
**(1664). Ainsty** [218/215](100).

***Association Oath Roll*, 1695** [C.213]
[316] **York.**

York City Archives, Art Gallery Building, Exhibition Square, York YO1 2EW.

***Hearth Tax***
**1665. York and Ainsty** [M30:22-23].
**1670. York** [M30:24]; **Ainsty** [E.80a].
**1671. York** [E80]. Typed transcript and index of persons (1,800).
**Ainsty** [M30:25].
**1674. York and Ainsty** [M30:26].

***Subsidy Rolls**, etc.* (all **York**)
**1665.** Micklegate ward [M30:5].
**1690.** Micklegate, Monk wards [M30:6-7].
**1691.** Bootham, Micklegate, Walmgate, Monk wards [M30:8-14].
**1692.** Walmgate ward [M30:15].
**1693.** St Wilfrid's parish [M30:16].

***Poll Tax***
**1690. York and Ainsty** [M30:20,21].
**1695-6. York,** St Martin Coney parish only (also described as 'Land Tax') [M30:31].
**No date,** c.**1694. York,** Christ's Parish and Minster Yard with Bedern [M30:30].

***Association Oath Roll*, 1695**
Council, gentry, clergy, citizens of **York** [M30:32].

## Yorkshire: East Riding

Publication

*Marriage Tax*, ***1695, 1697, Hull*** [Hull C.R.O. CAT.91-99] in *The People of Hull in 1695 and 1697: An index to the poll tax assessments* (not in fact a poll tax). 1695 excl. Humber ward.
1697 excl. St Mary's and North wards.

Public Record Office [E.179]

***Free and Voluntary Present*, 1661-2**
**Holderness wap.** [205/513](750).

***Hearth Tax*** *(Assessments and returns)*
(Microfilm available at Humberside R.O.)

**1662-3. Holderness** (mainly) [261/4] (?1,500). Miscellaneous paper returns from constables.
**(?1664). East Riding** [261/5](?1,500). Considerable decay, not repaired, also fading.
**Hull** [205/499](1,200).
**(1667). East Riding** [205/501](3,000). Increases and decreases of taxable hearths. Some decay, repaired, some fading.
**(1670). East Riding** [205/514](17,000). Slight decay at edges, not repaired. Includes exempt poor.
**1672. East Riding** [205/504](15,000). Loose ms., formerly sewn at head. Occasional decay, repaired.
**1673L&M. Hull** [205/505](1,500). Some decay, not repaired, mostly OK.
**1673-74.** Ten paper books, all VG, annotated and showing exempt poor:
**1673. Holderness wap.** [205/518](1,500).
**1673M & 1674L. Harthill wap.** [205/519] (1,050).
**1674. Holderness wap.** [205/520](1,150).
**1674L. Dickering wap.** [205/521](2,000).
**1673M & 1674L. Buckrose wap.** [205/522] (2,000).
**1673M & 1674L. Harthill wap., Bainton Beacon** [205/523](1,150).
**prob. 1674. Harthill wap., Hunsley Beacon** [205/524](1,250). Some pages fragile.
**prob. 1674. Beverley** [205/525](650).
**1674L. Howdenshire wap.** [261/9](900).
**1673M & 1674L. Ouse and Derwent wap.** (with Hull)[261/10](1,500).
**1675. East Riding** [261/11](?15,000).
*(Arrears)*(see also page 53)
**1663. East Riding** [205/493](200) and [205/495](450).
**1664. Hull** [261/6](200). By ward.
**1665M. East Riding** [205/502](5,000).

**Yorkshire, East Riding:** P.R.O. contd.

***Subsidies***

**1663. Harthill wap., Holme Beacon** [205/492](50). Badly decayed fragment, repaired, legibility variable.
**(1664). Hull** [205/494](225).
**Holderness wap.** [205/497](?150). Badly decayed, repaired, but most names lost, and legibility poor.
**Howdenshire wap.** [205/498](150).
**Harthill wap., Bainton Beacon** [205/467](150).

***Poll Tax** or **Aids***

**(1660). Hull** [205/486](1,250). Mainly OK, but 1m. faded.
**Holderness wap.** [205/487](750). Ms. sewn end to end.
**Holderness wap.** [205/488](1,000). VG.
**Hull, Humber ward** [205/489](300).
**Hull, Austin ward** [205/490](750).
**Hull** [205/460](250). Variable legibility.
**1667. East** and **West Ridings** [261/7] (?500-1,000). Schedules of defaulters. Two bundles, ms. of varying size.
**(1677). Hull** [205/484](700). VG.

***Association Oath Rolls*, 1695** [C.213] [317-18] **Hull;** [323] **Hedon;** [330] **Holderness.**
*See also under* **'Yorkshire'.**

Humberside Record Office, County Hall, Beverley, North Humberside HU17 9ba.

Microfilm available of P.R.O. holdings of *Hearth Tax* returns.

Kingston upon Hull City Record Office, 79 Lowgate, Kingston upon Hull HU1 2AA.

***Free and Voluntary Present*, 1661-2** [CAT.35] for all town.

***Aids**, etc.*

**1661.** Disbanding forces [CAT.37-42]. All town.
**1677.** [CAT.43-44]. One ward of town, two townships in county.
**1678.** [CAT.45-56]. Five wards of town, five townships in county.
**1678/9.** [CAT.57-67]. Five wards of town, six townships of county.
**1679/80.** [CAT. 68-75]. Four wards of town, four townships of county.
**1689-92.** [CAT.76-90]. Each year, some town wards only.

***Marriage Tax*** [CAT.91-99]
**1695, 1697.** Published, see left.

## Yorkshire: North Riding

Publication

*Hearth Tax* **1673** for **Downholme and Walburn** in Hangwest wap. [P.R.O. E.179/216/463](38) in 'The Hearth Tax and other records', by R. Fieldhouse, in *Group Projects in Local History*, ed. A. Rogers, 1977.

Public Record Office [E.179]

***Hearth Tax*** *(Assessments and returns)*

**1662M. North Riding** [215/451](22,200).
**North Riding** [215/452](22,200). Duplicate of 215/451. Richmond town excluded.
Terrington parish [245/20](62). Paper.
**1663L. Bulmer wap.** [261/23](?2,000). Constables' paper returns, variable condition.
**(1663). Hallikeld wap.** [215/455](1,200). Includes exempt poor.
**1664L. Pickering Lythe wap.** [261/27] (?1,000). Constables' paper returns.
**(1664). Bulmer wap.** [216/458](8,000). Includes exempt poor.
**(1667). North Riding** [216/460](8,250). Increases and decreases.
**(?1667). North Riding** [216/473](10,000). Increases and decreases. Parts badly decayed, not repaired, and faded. Poor legibility.
**Bulmer, Birdforth, East and West Hang, West Gilling waps., Allertonshire lib.** [261/26](5,000). Much fading, poor legibility.
**1670. North Riding** [216/461](32,000). Opening ms. faded, but most OK. Exempt poor shown.
**1671. West Gilling wap.** [261/28](250). Papers, bound together.
**(?1671). North Riding** [261/29](300). Schedule of variations. Flat. Much decay, not repaired.
**pre-1673. Birdforth wap.** [261/33](1,800). Flat.
**1673(?). North Riding** [216/462](22,500). Exempt poor shown. Microfilm of Birdforth, Allertonshire, Gilling East with John Hebden, transcript in progress.
**1673-74.** Five paper books, all including exempt poor:
**1673. Bulmer wap.** [216/481](3,100).
**1673. Allertonshire lib.** [216/482] (1,050).
**1673/4. Ryedale wap.** [216/483](2,250).
**1673M & 1674L. Hallikeld wap.** [216/484] (1,025).
**1673. East Gilling wap.** [261/30](1,350).

**Yorkshire, North Riding:**
P.R.O., *Hearth Tax*, continued

**1674. Birdforth, Hang, West Gilling, Langbaurgh, Pickering Lythe waps.** and **Whitby lib.** [261/32](?8,000). Paper returns by constables, repaired, bound.
**(1678). North Riding** (part) [216/470] (?250). Schedule of exemptions. Much lost from decay, repaired, and fading, but parts are legible.
**No date. Allertonshire lib.** [216/469] (1,200). Including exempt poor.
**East Gilling wap.** [216/471](1,500). Exempt poor shown.
**East Hang wap.** [216/472](1,150). Exempt poor shown.
**West Hang wap.** [216/474](2,000). Exempt poor shown.
**West Gilling wap.** [261/34](2,700).
**Langbaurgh wap.** [261/35](5,000). Exempt poor shown.
**Bulmer wap.** [249/4]. Huntington only.
*(Arrears)*(see also page 53)
**1663L. North Riding** [374/13](400). Latin. Desperate.

***Subsidies***
**1660. Great Ormsby** [239/233](80). Perhaps Aid, not Subsidy.
**(1663). Bulmer wap.** [215/453](350).
**Hallikeld wap./Richmondshire** [216/457] (100). Variable condn. and legibility.
**Langbaurgh wap.** [261/24](400).
**(1664). Bulmer wap.** [215/454](?150). Badly decayed, repaired; much lost.
**Pickering Lythe wap.** and **Whitby lib.** [216/456](55). Some decay and fading.
**Allertonshire lib.** [261/25](200).
**1673. Scarborough** [261/31](70). ? date.
**No date. West Gilling wap.** [216/477] (100). Badly decayed and faded.

***Association Oath Rolls*, 1695** [C.213] [320] **Scarborough;** [322] **Richmond;** [325] **Thirsk;** [326] **Northallerton.**
*See also under* **'Yorkshire'**.

North Yorkshire County Record Office, County Hall, Northallerton DL7 8SG.

***Marriage Tax*: Richmond, 1697-1705.** List of actual births, etc., on which tax was paid.

## Yorkshire: West Riding

Publications

'Return of the *Hearth Tax* for the **Wapentake of Skyrack, 1672'** [P.R.O. E.179/210/417], contr. by John Stansfield, *Miscellanea*, Thoresby Soc., vol.2, pt.3, 1891, pp.180-204, Aberforth - Leeds, Kirkgate (2,000), indexed; and vol.4, pt.1, 1892, pp.17-36, Leeds, Briggate - Yeadon (1,750), indexed.

*Hearth Tax*, **Leeds, 1663** [Leeds Corporation Court Book, LC/M1 p.212 foll., Leeds Archives](1,500) in *The Municipal History of the Borough of Leeds*, by James Wardell, 1846, pp. lxxxii-cxiii. Not indexed.

*Hearth Tax*, **Knaresborough, Bilton cum Harrogate, Pannall, 1664L** (wrongly described as 1676) [P.R.O. E.179/210/393] in *Records of Harrogate*, ed. Walter J. Kaye, 1922, Appendix 7.

*The Hearth Tax Returns of **1672L** for the **Wakefield** Metropolitan District* [from orig. in Wakefield M.D. Library] (2,500), trans. by Mrs J.A. Bottomley and Miss Dorothy Petyt, *Wakefield Hist. Soc. Journal*, vol.5, 1978. Arranged in alphabetical order of township. Orig. omits Pontefract. Not indexed.

*Hearth Tax*, **Sheffield, 1672L** [probably from Wakefield M.D. Library copy](527) in *The Flowing Stream* (Sheffield FHS), vol.2, pt.3, p.65, pt.4, pp.101-2; vol. 3, pt.1, pp.24-5, pt.2, pp.46-7 (1980-1). Preceded by 'A Brief Guide to the Records: Hearth Tax Returns'. Not indexed.

Public Record Office [E.179]

***Hearth Tax*** *(Assessments and returns)*
(Microfilm of returns relating to **Strafforth and Tickhill wapentake** at Sheffield Central Library.)

**1662M. Ripon lib.** [210/386](1,000). VG.
**Leeds borough** [262/9](?1,500). Bad decay, not repaired. Condition too bad to examine.
**1664L. West Riding** [210/393](32,000). Includes exempt poor.
**1664M. Barkstone wap.** [210/392](800). Supplementary assessment.
**1666L. Agbrigg and Morley waps.** [210/394a](8,800). Paper book. VG.
**Skyrack wap.** [210/421](4,000). Some decay, repaired. Incl. exempt poor.
**Claro wap.** [262/11](3,250). Paper book.
**1670M. West Riding** [210/411](27,500). Some decay at feet of ms., repaired.
**West Riding** [262/12](1,120). Schedule of empty houses and certified exempt.

**Yorkshire, West Riding:**
P.R.O., *Hearth Tax*, continued

**(prob. 1670M). Staincross, Osgoldcross and Staincliffe waps.** [210/414, part of 210/411](600). Badly decayed and faded, not repaired.

**(1670). Sheffield** [210/396](350). Sewn head to foot.

**1671. West Riding** [210/399](3,900). Variations in assessments. Interesting annotations.

**1672L. Claro wap.** [210/400](5,000). Very long ms. Including exempt poor. Indexed transcript from m'film by John Hebden for publication by Ripon FHS.

**Staincliffe** and **Ewcross waps.** [210/418] (5,500). Including exempt poor.

**Strafforth and Tickhill wap.** [262/15] (5,500). Very long ms. Microfilm at Sheffield Central Library. Indexed transcript at Doncaster Archives Dept. Sheffield section published.

**Prob. 1672L. Barkstone wap.** [262/14](2,500).

**(1672). Staincross wap.** [210/412] (1,500). Very long ms.

**Agbrigg and Morley waps.** [210/413] (?20,000).

**Osgoldcross wap.** [210/415](?2,500). Not checked in detail because of bad condition.

**Skyrack wap.** [210/417](3,750). Incl. exempt poor. Published, see left.

**1674L. West Riding** [262/13](35,000).

**No date. West Riding** [262/17](?5,000). Fragments, repaired and stitched into one roll. Very miscellaneous. Bad condition and legibility.

*(Arrears)*

**1663L. West Riding** [210/388b](900). Some fading.

**1663M. West Riding** [210/388a](800). VG.

**1662M-1664L (1665-6). West Riding and York** [210/394](3,000). Arrears schedule of the three Sheriffs of Yorks. and of York city. Latin. Variable legibility.

***Subsidies***

**1663. Strafforth wap.** and **Tickhill lib.** [210/390](750). Some decay, repaired. Some fading. Modern contents list.

**(1663). Claro wap.** [210/387](600). Some slight decay.

**1664. Staincross wap.** [210/301](200). Some decay, repaired. Variable leg.

**Agbrigg and Morley waps.** [262/10](900).

**Yorkshire: West Riding:**
P.R.O., *Subsidies*, continued

**1664/5. Strafforth wap.** and **Tickhill lib.** [210/389](750). Considerable fading. Modern contents list.

***Association Oath Rolls*, 1695** [C.213] [315] **Otley**; [319] **Knaresborough**; [321] **Ripon**; [324] **New Malton**; [327] **Pontefract**; [328] **Doncaster**; [329] **Leeds**; [331] Corporation of Cutlers (all Yorkshire).

*See also under* **'Yorkshire'**, page 50.

Leeds District Archives (West Yorkshire Archive Service), Chapeltown Road, Sheepscar, Leeds LS7 3AP.

***Hearth Tax***

**Leeds, 1663** [Leeds Corporation Court Book, LC/M1 p.212 foll.](1,500). Published, see left.

**Bramley** (Leeds) **1666**, MS copy [MD 10].

***Land Tax***

Sprotborough (incl. Newton and part of Cusworth), 1677, 1692, 1701, 1703 [BW/R 33].

Dacre, no date (temp.Anne)[Ingilby 3026].

Wakefield Metropolitan District Library

***Hearth Tax*** *(original)*

**West Riding, 1672L.** Omits Pontefract. Wakefield and Sheffield areas published, see left. Indexed by place.

Sheffield Central Library, Archives Division

Microfilm of *Hearth Tax* returns relating to **Strafforth and Tickhill wapentake**, i.e., most of South Yorkshire.

Doncaster Archives Dept., King Edward Road, Balby, Doncaster, S.Yks. DN4 ONA.

***Hearth Tax*** *(transcript)*

**1672L. Lower Strafforth and Tickhill wap.** [from P.R.O. E.179/262/15] (2,500+). Indexed in main name index.

***Marriage Tax*** *(originals)*

**Doncaster, 1706** [AB.6/1/21](100+).

***Land Tax*** *(originals)*

**Doncaster** Township **1700, 1703, 1710, 1712**; Soke **1702-3** (some parishes); Blaxton **1712** [AB.6/2/11].

***Window Tax*** *(originals)*

Various townships, **1700-12** [AB.6/2/10]. These give the amount payable, but not the number of windows.

# WALES

## Anglesey

Public Record Office [E.179]

***Hearth Tax*** *(Assessments and returns)* (Transcripts at U.C.N.W., Bangor)

**1662M. County** [263/5](?2,300). Much decay and fading. 219/26 is based on this list and is better preserved. Introduction and detailed contents list by CAFM.
**1664M. County** [219/26](2,300). 1662M return for use 1664M, annotated. VG.
**1670M. County** [219/27](2,750). Exempt poor shown. Beaumaris by streets. VG, but 1m. lost. Dated 2 May 1671.
**1673M. County** [219/28](3,250). Exempt poor shown. Dated 8 Oct 1674.
*(Arrears)*
**1662M. County** [219/25](100). Some decay.
**1663M. County** [219/24](250).

***Association Oath Rolls*, 1695** [C.213] [333] **Anglesey**; [334] **Beaumaris.**

Department of Manuscripts, The Library, University College of North Wales, Bangor, Gwynedd LL57 2DG.

Leonard Owen transcripts: ***Hearth Tax***
**1662M, 1664M, 1673M, County** [Bangor MS. 10252, from P.R.O. E.179/263/5, 219/26,28].
**1662M, 1664M, 1670M, 1673M. County** [Bangor MS.13970, from P.R.O. E.179/ 263/5, 219/26, 219/28, 219/27].

National Library of Wales (Dept. of MSS), Aberystwyth, Dyfed SY23 3BU.

***Marriage Tax*** [Carreglwyd collection]
Coedana, 1695 [369]; Llanbabo, 1695-7 [2315]; Clegyrog, parish of Llanbadrig, 1698 [848]; Llanbadrig, 1704 [760]; Llanfaes, 1701 [492]; Llanfair-yng-Nghornwy, 1700 [810]; Llanfigel, 1695-1697 [1848], 1703-4 [2241]; Llanrhwy-drys, 1698-9 [1416], 1700 [912]; Llan-fachreth, 1695-7 [1847], 1699 [846], 1701-2 [532], 1704 [2201]; Llanfwrog, 1703-4 [280]; Hundred of Llifon and Talybolion, 1698-9 [1463]; Hundred of Talybolion, 1704 [1417].

***Aid/Land Tax***
**Talybolion hd., 1693-4, 1706, 1709** [Carreglwyd 98, 1191, 258, 221].

## Breconshire

Public Record Office [E.179]

***Free and Voluntary Present*, 1661-2**
**County** [263/27](3,100).

***Hearth Tax*** *(Assessments and returns)*

**1664L. County** [263/28](5,000). Sewn head to foot, awkward to consult. Much fading, poor legibility.
**No date. County** [219/63](5,100). Good Includes exempt poor.

***Aid or Poll Tax***
**No date. County** [263/29](1,600). Some decay at feet of ms.

***Association Oath Rolls*, 1695** [C.213] [335-37] **County**; [338] **Brecon.**

## Caernarvonshire

Public Record Office [E.179]

***Hearth Tax*** *(Assessments and returns)*

**?1662M, 1670M. County** [368/10]( ? ). Fragments, bad condition and legibility.
*(Arrears)*
**1671. County** (with Montgomery)[263/1] (150). Paper book, poor condition.

***Subsidies***
**1663/4. County** [220/161](150). Flat. Some fading. Transcript at U.C.N.W.

***Association Oath Rolls*, 1695** [C.213] [344] **County**; [345] **Caernarvon**; [346] **Maynal Bangor.**

Caernarfon Area Record office (Gwynec Archives Service), County Offices, Shirehall Street, Caernarfon LL55 1SI

***Hearth Tax*** *(original)*
**(No date,** probably **1662M). County.** Tr script at U.C.N.W., Bangor, below.

Department of Manuscripts, The Librai University College of North Wales, Bangor, Gwynedd LL57 2DG.

Leonard Owen transripts:
*Hearth Tax* (prob. **1662M**). **County** [Ban MS.13491, from Caernarfon R.O. ori
*Subsidy*, **1663/4. County** [Bangor MS.13 from P.R.O. E.179/220/161](150).

## Cardiganshire

Public Record Office [E.179]

***Free and Voluntary Present*, 1661-2**
**County** [263/43](3,000).

***Hearth Tax*** *(Assessments and returns)*
**1670L. County** [219/94](5,000). Includes exempt poor. VG.
**1672M. County** [219/95](2,500).
**No date** (prob. **1670**'s). **County** [263/46] (5,300). Short ms. Exempt poor shown.
*(Arrears)*
**1662M. County** [219/90a](100). Latin.
**1663M. County** [219/91-3](350). Latin.
**1671M-1673L. County** [224/599]. 1671M for 1 yr (140), 1673L for 1½ yrs (150). Paper books.

***Subsidy***
**(1664). County** [263/44](300).

***Aid***
**(?1666). County** [263/45](300).

***Association Oath Rolls*, 1695** [C.213] [339-40] **County.**

## Carmarthenshire

Public Record Office [E.179]

***Free and Voluntary Present*, 1661-2**
**Carmarthen** [264/15](250).
**Cathinog hd.** [264/16](250).
**Cayo, Derllys** and **Kidwelly hds.** [264/17] (?1,000). Partly paper, fragile.
**Elvet hd.** [264/18](500).
**Perfedd hd.** [264/19](300).

***Hearth Tax*** *(Assessments and returns)*

**1670M. County** [220/128](4,850). For 1½ years.
**(prob. 1670s). County** [264/22](8,000). Flattened ms. Slight decay at feet of ms. Considerable fading and much poor legibility. Exempt poor shown.
*(Arrears)*
**1663L. Carmarthen** borough [375/9,10] (110). Sperate and desperate. Latin.
**1664L. County** [264/21](150). Latin. Desperate.
**1671M-1673M. County** [224/599]. Two paper books, 1671M, 1 yr (375); 1673M, 1½ years (420).

***Poll Tax*** *(?)*
**(No date, W&M). County** [220/130](1,250).

***Association Oath Rolls*, 1695** [C.213] [341] **County**; [342] **Carmarthen**; [343] **Langham.**

## Denbighshire

Publication

*Hearth Tax Arrears, Desperate*, **1663M** [P.R.O. E.179/221/205](350 collectors), *Hel Achau* (Clwyd FHS) **13**, Summer 1984, pp.9-12, as 'Hearth Tax Assessment for **Isaled Commote**', by William A. Morris.

Public Record Office [E.179]

***Hearth Tax*** *(Assessments and returns)*

**1664L. County** [264/36](?10,000). Much decay, fading; very poor legibility.
**1666L. County** [221/299]. Six paper books, annotated, VG. 1, 3 and 4 are fair copies of 6. Transcript of 1-5 at U.C.N.W., Bangor, see below.
1. **Bromfield hd.** (3,400);
2. **Ychdilas/Isdulas hd.** (2,000);
3. **Ruthen and Yale hd.** (2,500);
4. **Chirke hd.** (1,700);
5. **Issallet/Isaled hd.** (1,850);
6. **Yale, Bromfield** and **Chirk hds.** (7,600).

**1671M. County** (and Flint)[263/2] (?1,200). Particulars of variations. Some decay, much fading, poor leg. Issallet and Ychdilas hds. missing.
**No date. Bromfield hd.** [264/35](1,250). Paper book, probably rough copy.

***Association Oath Rolls*, 1695** [C.213] [347-48] **County.**

Dept. of MSS., The Library, University College of North Wales, Bangor LL57 2DG.

Leonard Owen transcripts: ***Hearth Tax***
**1666L. County** [Bangor MS.13493, from P.R.O. E.179/221/299].

## Flintshire

Public Record Office [E.179]

***Hearth Tax*** *(Assessments and returns)*

**1664M. County** [221/230](4,750). Some ms. badly decayed, repaired, mostly OK. Annotated; includes exempt poor. Intro. by CAFM. M/f at Clwyd R.O. Transcript at U.C.N.W., Bangor.
**1670M. County** [264/45](6,000). Some decay, repaired, staining and loss of legibility, but mostly OK. Exempt poor shown. M/f and transcript at Clwyd R.O. Transcript also at U.C.N.W., Bangor.
**1671M. County** (and Denbighs.)[263/2]. Variations. See under Denbighshire.

***Association Oath Rolls*, 1695** [C.213] [349] **County**; [350] **Flint.**

**Flintshire**, continued

Clwyd Record Office, The Old Rectory, Hawarden, Deeside, Clwyd CH5 3NR.

***Hearth Tax***
Microfilms of **1664M** [P.R.O. E.179/221/230] and **1670M** [E.179/264/45].
Transcript of **1670M** [NT/61, from P.R.O. E.179/264/45].

Department of Manuscripts, The Library, University College of North Wales, Bangor, Gwynedd LL57 2DG.

Leonard Owen transcripts [Bangor MS. 13971]: ***Hearth Tax***
**1664M. County** [from P.R.O. E.179/221/230].
**1670M. County** [from E.179/264/45].

## Glamorgan

Public Record Office [E.179]

***Free and Voluntary Present***, **1661-2**
**County** [264/47](?5,000).

***Hearth Tax*** *(Assesments and returns)*
(Microfilms of asterisked records at Glamorgan Archive Service, Cardiff)

**1670M. County** [221/294]*(8,900). Exempt poor shown.
**1672M. Miskin hd.** [221/295]*(600).
**1672. Dinas Powis hd.** [375/6](1,200). Some decay, repaired.
**(1672). Ogmore hd.** [221/298](80). Fragment. Flattened ms. Decay repaired. Some names illegible, others OK.
**Swansea hd.** [375/7](50). Fragment.
**No date. County** [221/297]*(9,600). Flattened ms. Includes exempt poor.
**Caerphilly hd.** [221/296]*(600).
**Neath hd.** [264/48](500).
*(Arrears)*
**1664L. County** [221/290]*(80). Latin.
**1671M-1673L. County** [224/599]*. Two paper books. 1671M, 1 year (520), 1672M-1673L, 1½ years (500).

***Aid***
**No date. County** [276/47B](650).

***Association Oath Roll***, **1695** [C.213] [351] **County.**

Glamorgan Archive Service, County Hall, Cathays Park, Cardiff CF1 3NE.

***Hearth Tax***
Microfilm of **1671, 1673** [P.R.O. E.179/221/290; 221/294-297; 224/599].

## Merionethshire

Publication

'The *Hearth Tax* of **1662M** in **Merioneth**, [P.R.O. E.179/265/2](1,950), by Owen Parry, *Jnl. of the Merioneth Historical and Record Soc. (Clychgrawn Cwmdeithas Hanes a Chofnodion Sir Feironnydd)*, vol.2, pt.1, 1953-6, pp.16-38. Lists compiled by petty and high constables. Missing: Ystumaner, Llanbedr, Llanfihangel, Llanfrothen and Llanaber in Ardydwy. Not indexed.

Public Record Office [E.179]

***Hearth Tax*** *(Assessments and returns)*

**1662M. County** [265/2](1,950). Published. Some decay, repaired, considerable staining and some poor legibility, but mostly OK.
**1666L. County** [222/400a](4,500). Paper book, annotated. Parry comments: 'names anglicized, work of a stranger'. Transcript at U.C.N.W., Bangor.
*(Arrears)*
**1663M. County** [375/39](100).

***Subsidy***
**(1663). County** [222/331](300). Sewn head to foot. Transcript at U.C.N.W.

***Aid***
**(1664-6). County** [222/332](?500-1,000). Transcript at U.C.N.W.

***Association Oath Roll***, **1695** [C.213] [352] **County.**

Dept. of MSS., The Library, University College of North Wales, Bangor LL57 2DG.

Leonard Owen transcripts [Bangor MS. 13494]:

***Hearth Tax***
**1666L. County** [from P.R.O. E.179/222/400a]

***Subsidy***
**(1663). County** [from E.179/222/331].

***Aid***
**(1664-6). County** [from E.179/222/332].

**Note.** *Local Population Studies*, **20** (Spring 1978), pp.63-64, lists 2 parishes in Caernarvonshire, 32 in Denbighshire, 20 in Flintshire and 11 in Merionethshire for which there are population lists, mainly **1680-1** (*not* tax assessments). Photocopies of these are at the Cambridge Group for Population Studies, 27 Trumpington Street, Cambridge CB2 1QA.

## Montgomeryshire

Public Record Office

*Hearth Tax (Assessments and returns)*
(Transcripts at U.C.N.W. Bangor.)

**1662M. County** [265/7](6,000). Some decay, repaired, considerable fading and staining, some poor legibility, but mostly OK. Introduction and detailed contents list by CAFM.
**1671, County** [265/10](6,200). Exempt poor shown. Transcript at Soc of Gen.
*(Arrears)*
**1663M. County** [265/9](50). Latin.
**1671. County** (with Caernarvonshire) [263/1](250). Paper book.

***Subsidies***
(Transcripts at U.C.N.W., Bangor.)
**1663. County** [265/8](300). Flat. Considerable decay, not repaired; some fading.
**(1667). Deythur, Llanfyllin, Machynlleth, Mathrafel** and **Pool hds.** [223/403] (200). Bad decay, repaired. Many names lost.

***Poll Tax***
**(1665-6). County** [223/405](1,700). Transcript at U.C.N.W., Bangor.
**(1697). County** [223/406](150). Collectors' names only.

***Association Oath Rolls*, 1695** [C.213] [353] **County**; [354] **Montgomery**; [355] **Welshpool.**

Department of Manuscripts, The Library, University College of North Wales, Bangor, Gwynedd LL57 2DG.

Leonard Owen transcripts [Bangor MS. 13974]:

***Hearth Tax***
**1662M. County** [from P.R.O. E.179/265/7].
**1671. County** [from E.179/265/10].

***Subsidies***
**1663. County** [from P.R.O. E.179/265/8].
**(1667). Deythur, Llanfyllin, Machynlleth, Mathrafel** and **Pool hds.** [from P.R.O. E.179/223/403].

***Poll Tax***
**(1665-6). County** [from P.R.O. E.179/223/405].

Society of Genealogists, 14 Charterhouse Buildings, Goswell Rd, London EC1M 7BA.

*Hearth Tax:* **1671. County** [from P.R.O. E.179/265/10]. TS transcript. Not indexed. Wrongly described as 1680.

## Pembrokeshire

Publications

*Hearth Tax*, **1670M, County** [P.R.O. E.179/224/532 except for m.44], in 'Pembrokeshire Hearths in 1670', *West Wales Historical Records*. Exempt poor shown. Excludes Haverfordwest. Not indexed.
**Vol.9** (1920-23), pp.217-40: Kilgarron hd.; Roose hd.(part)(1,700).
**Vol.10** (1924), pp.177-216: Roose hd., ctd.; Castlemartin, Dongleddy hds.; Dewsland hd. (part)(3,000).
**Vol.11** (1926), pp.113-40: Dewsland hd., ctd.; Narberth hd. (1,600).

Public Record Office [E.179]

***Free and Voluntary Present*, 1661-2**
**County** [265/18](2,400). Ms. head to foot.

***Hearth Tax** (Assessments and returns)*

**1670M. County** [224/532](6,300). Published.
**1671M. County** [375/41](?6,500). In six parts. Much decay, repaired, and fading. Legibility variable.
*(Arrears)*
**1671M-1673L. County** [224/599]. Two paper books. 1671M (500); 1673L (500).

***Subsidy** or **Aid**(?)*
**(1666). County** [224/530](680). Flat.

***Association Oath Rolls*, 1695** [C.213] [356-57] **County**; [358] **Pembroke**; [359] **Haverfordwest**; [360] **Tenby.**

Pembrokeshire Record Office (Dyfed Archives), The Castle, Haverfordwest.

**Haverfordwest:** *Poll Tax*, **1698**; *Window Tax*, **1707** (St Mary s only); *Land Tax*, **1698-1721.**

## Radnorshire

Public Record Office [E.179]

***Free and Voluntary Present*, 1661-2**
**County** [265/22](2,500).

***Hearth Tax** (Assessments and returns)*

**No date. County** [224/593](3,600). Short ms. Includes exempt poor.
[265/23](150). Fragments, for Llanbister, Llanbadarn, Broylis only. Exempt poor shown. Some fading, some decay, not repaired.

***Aid***
**(1666). County** [224/591](250).

***Association Oath Rolls*, 1695** [C.213] [361-63] **County**; [364] **Radnor.**

## SCOTLAND

Although Scotland was of course not subject to taxes levied by the English parliament, there were similar taxes during the later Stuart period. Chief amongst these were the ***Hearth Tax*** of **1691** and the ***Poll Tax*** Rolls, **1694-1699**. These have been briefly described in *Sources for Scottish Genealogy and Family History*, D.J. Steel (*National Index of Parish Registers*, vol.12), 1970, pp.121-24, 171-74 (based on articles by J.F. Mitchell and William Rodger first published in the *Scottish Genealogist*, **10**, 4 and **11**, 3, 1964). However, since then the Scottish Record Society has published an authoritative volume relating to the Hearth Tax, on which much of the information given here is, by kind permission, based.

***Hearth Tax***

This tax is fully described and discussed in *West Lothian Hearth Tax **1691**; with county abstracts for Scotland*, ed. Duncan Adamson, Scottish Record Society, N.S. **9**, 1981. Although its collection in some cases took several years, the tax was levied in relation to 1691, and the names listed are those who were the householders on Candlemas day, 1691. In some cases, however, usually towns, the lists instead refer to the autumn of 1690. The records are all now in the Scottish Record Office, H.M. General Register House, Edinburgh EH1 1EW.

The only returns published are those for Dumfriesshire, southern Perthshire and Stirlingshire, and West Lothian.

The second part of the S.R.S. volume describes, county by county, the returns for each, giving the name of the sub-collector; the 'Nature of Record': a detailed description of the content of the returns and geographical arrangement; the S.R.O. reference; date it was deponed; a list of all parishes/places, in the order in which they appear, and their number of hearths; and the total number of hearths. In the county entries that follow, the S.R.O. references are shown in square brackets and the number of hearths (**not** householders) in round brackets, both taken from the S.R.S. volume.

***Poll Tax*, 1694-1699**

The most accessible description of this important record is probably that by D.J. Steel in *Sources for Scottish Genealogy and Family History*, pp.121-24. Amount of detail varies, but at best all the household may be named. The records for which references are given are in the Scottish Record Office unless shown otherwise. Published transcripts are given under county entries.

**HT** = Hearth Tax; **PT** = Poll Tax.

**Aberdeenshire**: **HT** [E69/1-12](27,102 - but totals only, no names).

**PT**: *List of Pollable Persons within the Shire of Aberdeen, **1696***, pub. 1844, 2 vols. All parishes [Aberdeen Univ. Archives MS.548]. New edition by Aberdeen & NE Scotland FHS: Lonmay, Old Deer & Long Side, Aberdeen & Freedom Lands, Peterculter, Strathbogie (2 vols.) pubd. Remainder in preparation.

**1694**. Kearn [GD.52/6].

**1698**. Alford, Tough, Leochel, Cushnie, Tullynessle, Forbes, Kearn, Clatt and Kennethmont [GD.52/7].

**1699**. Same parishes [GD.52/8].

Angus - see Forfarshire.

**Argyll and Bute**: **HT** [E69/3; GD1112/10/10 (Breadalbane papers)](6,539 - names given, except for Mull, Tiree, Coll, Ardnamurchan, Sunart, Appin, Glencoe, Canna and Morvern, 'being in rebellion').

**PT** [Records from the Argyll Sheriff Court, now in West Register House]:

**1698**. Islay [SC/54/19/44/3].

**1699**. Kilfinnan, Kintyre, Kilmichael-Glassary and Kilmartin [SC/54/19/44/4,6,7]. Very few names in either.

**Ayrshire**: **HT**. Carrick [E69/2/2](2,339 - taxpayers' names only); Kyle [E69/2/1] (5,836 - variable record of taxpayers' names); Cunningham [E69/2/3](5,750 - taxpayers' names).

**PT. 1698**. Largs [E70/1(2)].

**1699**. Barr, Dailly, Girvan [E70/1(1)]. Very few names in either.

**Banffshire**: **HT** [E69/4/1-2](3,249 - but totals only, no names).

**PT**: List of persons deficient in payment of PT of 1695, dated 1697 [Banffshire Sheriff Court Records]. Printed in *Transactions of Banffshire Field Club*, **24** (1903-4), pp.3-18.

*SCOTLAND*, continued

**Berwickshire: HT** [E69/5; GD26/7/359] (5,470 - taxpayers' names only).
**PT. 1695.** Ayton, Edrom, Eyemouth, Greenlaw, Polwarth [Fraser Charters GD/86/770A]. All give occupations and location of houses, Greenlaw also wives and children. Mitchell/Steel also lists Swinton, not on S.R.O. list.
Hutton [Hume of Marchmont collection, GD.158/679]. Names wives, children, occupations, location of houses.
Lauder [E70/2/1]. Very few names.

Bute - see Argyll.

**Caithness: HT** [GD26/7/373](3,348 - but totals only, no names).

**Clackmannanshire: HT** [E69/6](1,442 - of which 190 are un-named poor).

**Dumfriesshire: HT** [GD26/7](about 7,500). Tax lists and analysis (ed. Duncan Adamson) published in *Transactions of the Dumfries and Galloway Natural History Society*, vols.47-9 (1970-2).

**Dunbartonshire: HT** [E69/7](2,882 - names of householders, farm by farm, but total only for Dumbarton (282)).

**East Lothian: HT.** Haddington Presbytery [E69/9/2-4](8,733) - taxpayers named, but not 611 poor); Dunbar Presbytery [E69/9/1](1,947 - taxpayers named).
**PT. 1698.** Dirleton [E70/3]. Few names.

**Edinburgh and Leith: HT** [E69/16/2-3] (19,624 - individual names given).
**PT. 1694.** [E70/4/1-11]. Canongate (wives, occupations); College Kirk (wives); Greyfriars (wives, imperfect); Lady Yester's (wives, imperfect); New Kirk (children, imperfect); Old Kirk (children); West Kirk (St Cuthbert's (occupations, location of houses); North Leith (occupations); South Leith (imperfact); Tolbooth (wives, children, occupations); Tron Kirk (wives, children, occupations).
[Edinburgh Town Council records]:
**1694.** 1. Tolbooth; 2. Old Kirk. Published in *Edinburgh Poll Tax Returns for 1694*, ed. Marguerite Wood, Scottish Record Soc., 1951. Indexed. See also 'Edinburgh Poll Tax Returns' by Marguerite Wood, in *Book of the Old Edinburgh Club*, **25**, pp.90-120.
**1695.** 3-5. Old Kirk; Greyfriars; New Kirk;
**1698.** 6. Lady Yester's parish; 7. College Kirk; 8. New Kirk.
**1699.** 9. New Kirk.
*See also* Midlothian.

Elgin - see Moray.

**Fife and Kinross: HT.** Dunfermline Presbytery [E69/10/1](4,485 - of which 282 are un-named poor); Presyteries of St Andrews, Cuper and Kircaldy [E69/10/2](15,376 paid and named; 739 poor or deficient, un-named).
**PT. 1695-6.** Anstruther Wester [original in Anstruther Town Council records, transcript at S.R.O., RH.2/1/68]. Names wives, children, occupations.
**1698.** Aberdour, Wemyss [E70/5/1,2]. Very few names.
**No date.** St Andrews [original in St Andrews burgh records, B/65/20/2]; ? transcript at S.R.O.

**Forfarshire** (Angus)(including parts of modern Perthshire): **HT** [E69/11/1] (14,000 but often block estate totals rather than individual names).

Haddington - see East Lothian.

**Inverness-shire: HT** [E69/12/1](6,789 - generally in block totals, headed by heritors' names; names of 151 individual poor are given).
**PT. 1699.** Inverness burgh (118 names, occupation, location of houses); other places named: Brarban, Croy, Daviol, Moy, Dunlechity, Dallarsie, Durvis, Ballieskin, Abertariff, Urquhart and Glenmoriston, Ward Law, Kiltarlie, Killincrack(?), Strathspey, Rothiemurchis, Kingussie, Allowe, Culloden, Kilfinnan, Isle of Skye. [E70/6/1](156 names, excl. Inverness).

**Kincardineshire: HT** [E69/13](4,033 - of which 405 are un-named poor).

Kinross - see Fife.

**Stewartry of Kirkcudbright: HT** [E69/14] (3,364 - but block totals grouped by estate only, no names).

**Lanarkshire** (Clydesdale): **HT** [E69/15] (19,196 - but variable for detail. Some parishes give all names, some just those that paid. In the south, the record is very poor, usually in blocks under heritors. Some parishes, including Glasgow, give only total).
**PT. 1695.** Lesmahagow, published in *Annals of the Parish of Lesmahagow*, by J.B. Greenshields, 1864, pp.163-85. [Original in private collection; lists for the remainder of the Upper Ward of Lanarkshire existed mid-C19, but present location probably unknown].
Burgh of Glasgow, deficients only [E70/7/4].

*SCOTLAND:* **Lanarkshire**, *Poll Tax*, contd.

**1698.** Barony (Glasgow), Bothwell, Cadder, Cambuslang, Carmunnock, Govan, Lanark, Lesmahagow, Rutherglen [E70/7/1-3]. Very few names.
**1699–1700?** Burgh of Glasgow (incomplete)[E70/7/5].

Linlithgowshire - see West Lothian.

**Midlothian: HT** [E69/16/1](10,920 - but variable for detail. Individuals named in some parishes, block estate totals only for others).
**PT.** [E70/8]. (a = wives named; b = children named; c = occupations given; d = locations of houses given).
**1694.** Carrington (a,b,c); Cockpen (a, b,c), pubd. in *Scottish Genealogist*, **19**, 2 (June 1972), pp.63-8; Cramond (a,b,d); Cranston and Falla (c); Dalkeith and Lasswade (d), Lasswade pubd. in *Scot. Gen.*, **28**, 3 (Sept 81), pp.122-39; Duddingston (d); Inveresk (c); Kirknewton (c,d); Liberton (b,c, d); Newbattle (imperfect; a,b,c); Penicuik (b,c,d); Ratho (a,b,c,d); Stow (a,b,c,d); Temple (c).
**No date.** Borthwick (b,c,d); Colinton (imperfect; a,c); Crichton (b,c,d); Currie (imperfect; a,c); Calderclare or East Calder (d); Heriot (b,c); Mid Calder (b,c); West Calder (c,d).
*See also* Edinburgh. Leith and Canongate.

**Moray** (Elgin) **and Nairn: HT** [E69/17] (2,545 - but block totals only, no names).
**PT. 1698** [E70/9(1) 'List for shire']. Ardclach (7), Auldearn (14), Calder (6), Croy (3), Nairn (3).

**Orkney and Shetland. HT. Shetland** only [GD26/7/327](1,786 - but totals only, no names). None for Orkney.
**PT. 1695–6, Orkney** only [Orkney and Shetland collection (Register House), 2 vols. RH.9/15/175]. All parishes (wives, children, occupations, houses, for some parishes only).
**1698.** [E70/10(1)]. Kirkwall burgh.

**Peebles** - see with Selkirkshire

**Perthshire. HT.** Perth and Dunkeld Presbyteries [E69/1-4](15,371); Dunblane and Auchterarder Presbyteries with Culross and Tulliallan parishes: [? ref.](9,027). Southern Perthshire hearth books are includes with the gravestone survey published by the Scottish Genealogy Society.

**Perthshire**, continued

**PT. 1694.** [B59/22/24]. Perth burgh.
**1695.** [Rollo of Duncrub MSS, GD.56/128, Register House] Part of Dunning (Dalreoch and Ballgouer pertaining to the Laird of Gleneagles).
[Fergusson of Baledmund muniments.] Persons belonging to John Fergusson of Dunfallandie.
**1696.** [GD.316/10] Parish of Errol.

**Renfrewshire. HT** [E69/20](5,473 - individuals named except in Houston).
**PT. 1695.** All parishes in county [?formerly in Paisley Town Council records]. Publ. in *Glasgow Herald*, 1864. Copies of set of cuttings at Paisley Library (indexed); S.R.O. [T.335, Printed Books catalogue]; Glasgow University Library; Scottish Society of Antiquaries; and British Library.
**Kilmacolm** and **Kilbarchan** pub. by the New Society, vols. 10 and 12. **Paisley** in *A History of Paisley, 1660-1908*, by W.M. Metcalfe, 1909; **Kilbarchan** in *Kilbarchan: A Parish History*, R.D. Mackenzie, 1902; **Kilmacolm,** in *Kilmacolm*, J. Murray, 1907; **Neilston** in *History of the Parish of Neilston*, D. Pride, 1910.
**1694–6.** [E70/12]. Houston (children, occpns.); Inchinnan (imperfect; wives, children); Kilbarchan (wives, children, houses); Killellan (occpns., houses); Kilmacolm (wives, children, occpns.). These lists sometimes have material additional to that published.

**Ross and Cromarty: HT** [GD26/7/391] (3,695 - totals only, no names).

**Roxburghshire: HT** [E69/21](7,101 - of which 391 are un-named poor).

**Selkirkshire and Peebleshire** (Forest and Tweeddale): **HT** [E69/18](3,447 - but generally block totals under estates, no names).
**PT. 1694** [SC.42/5/1 . Peebles: Lintoun, Skurling, Barns, Cringellie, Blackbanonie, Countess of Mortoun, Haystoun.
Selkirks: [Horsburgh paper GD.178/box 2]. Selkirk, 1694, 1695 (?also Ettrick).
Shetland - see with Orkney.

**Stirlingshire: HT** [E69/22/1](8,114 - varies from a very detailed record for Stirling burgh to parishes which do not give individual names at all). Stirlingshire hearth books are included with the gravestone survey published by the Scottish Genealogy Society.